On Being Presidential

Susan Resneck Pierce

Foreword by Judith Block McLaughlin

On Being Presidential

A Guide for College and University Leaders

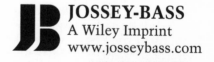

JOSSEY-BASS
A Wiley Imprint
www.josseybass.com

insidehighered.com

Published by Jossey-Bass

A Wiley Imprint

One Montgomery Street, Suite 1200, San Francisco, CA 94104-4594—

www.josseybass.com

Jossey-Bass books and products are available through most bookstores. To contact Jossey-Bass directly call our Customer Care Department within the U.S. at 800-956-7739, outside the U.S. at 317-572-3986, or fax 317-572-4002.

Wiley also publishes its books in a variety of electronic formats and by print-on-demand. Not all content that is available in standard print versions of this book may appear or be packaged in all book formats. If you have purchased a version of this book that did not include media that is referenced by or accompanies a standard print version, you may request this media by visiting http://booksupport.wiley.com. For more information about Wiley products, visit us at www.wiley.com.

Chapter Six, Letting Go and Leaving Gracefully, expands on "Toward a Smooth Presidential Transition" by Susan Resneck Pierce originally published in *Trusteeship* 11(5), p. 13–17.

Library of Congress Cataloging-in-Publication Data

Pierce, Susan Resneck, 1943–
    On being presidential : a guide for college and university leaders / Susan Resneck Pierce ; foreword by Judith Block McLaughlin. – 1st ed.
        p. cm. – (The Jossey-Bass higher and adult education series)
    Includes bibliographical referneces and index.
    ISBN 978-1-118-02776-9; ISBN 978-1-118-13317-0;
    ISBN 978-1-118-13318-7; ISBN 978-1-118-13320-0
    1. College presidents–United States.   2. Educational leadership–United States.   I. Title.
    LB2341.P54 2012
    378.1'11–dc23   2011029333

Printed in the United States of America

FIRST EDITION

HB *Printing* 10   9   8   7   6   5   4   3   2   1

Contents

Foreword

Many former presidents write memoirs describing their successes (and only occasionally their failures and shortcomings), offering advice based on their own experience. Although written by a president emeritus, this book moves well beyond the usual focus on one person in one institution. In addressing the challenges of presidential leadership, Susan Resneck Pierce benefits from many perspectives: from her own successful presidency to her post-presidential experience as a consultant to boards, presidents, and executive leadership teams. This book is a compendium of important insights and essential information for college and university presidents and for those who work closely with them.

Paradoxically, the book begins with a litany of presidential disasters, many of which are so obvious as to make you wonder how people smart enough to reach the college presidency could behave so stupidly. The answer is that their missteps represent an accumulation of errors in judgment, not just one. They are the consequence of the traps that all presidents face: the illusion of power; the seduction of flattery; and the slippage from curiosity and learning to impatience and certitude, and from self-confidence to arrogance.

Although organizational charts show the presidency as the apex position, successful presidents quickly learn that the ability to effect change does not come from positional power. They must engage in ongoing negotiations with multiple constituencies, have an awareness of the symbolic role of leadership, and empower others. Susan Pierce identifies many of the dilemmas that presidents encounter while trying to find the right balance points in the course of their work. How quickly should new presidents make major decisions? When should they, as well as longer-term presidents, consult with others or make decisions more quickly and independently? How can "shared governance" best be accomplished with the board of trustees and the faculty?

Susan Pierce offers wise counsel on all aspects of the presidency, from raising money to living in the "fishbowl"—both aspects of the job that newcomers find daunting. She offers compelling stories that capture the nuances of issues, and she gives pragmatic advice on how presidents can best traverse this complex terrain. Lest presidents or presidential aspirants grow discouraged by the many problems and predicaments they face, Pierce's chapter on the pleasures of the presidency provides a helpful antidote. I remember my experience as chair of the Harvard Seminar for New Presidents during its initial year in 1990, when many of the presenters tried to "lighten" their sessions by telling jokes about the travails of the presidency. About two-thirds of the way through the week, several new presidents came up to me and said that the job couldn't possibly be so bleak, could it, if these enormously capable presidents remained in it? From then on, I asked the presidents to talk more about the satisfactions of the position, something they readily agreed to do—because despite the very real challenges of the presidency, they loved their work. Pierce identifies many rewarding aspects of the job while also cautioning presidents to take their work but not themselves too seriously. As Stephen Sweeny, former president of the College of New Rochelle, has often advised new presidents in the Harvard Seminar, the presidency is "a privileged position, not a position of privilege."

Drawing upon her expertise as a search consultant, Pierce offers boards of trustees and presidential aspirants excellent advice on presidential searches. But one of this book's most important contributions is Pierce's discussion of the "other end" of the presidential transition, the presidential departure. Much less has been written on this crucial time, a passage fraught with hazards for individuals and institutions. Many presidents are unsure how to decide when it is time to leave. Longer-term presidents especially can have a hard time letting go. As Pierce explains cogently, the job has become their life and their identity. Staying on campus should not be an option, however. Although boards of trustees may consider this practice benign or even helpful to the new president, it is at best a complication and at worst a serious hindrance to the leadership of the new incumbent.

Very talented and capable people leave presidencies with still many productive years ahead of them. We would do well to think about how higher education, government, national higher education associations, foundations, and think tanks could benefit from this substantial base of experience. Susan Pierce is an excellent case in point. Since her presidency, she has improved colleges and universities by her consultancies. With this book, she shares her wisdom even more broadly, enriching our understanding of the many dimensions of the work and the life of college presidents.

Judith Block McLaughlin
Harvard Graduate School of Education

*In memory of Dory Resneck and Kenneth Pierce and for
Sean Derek Siegel and Ryan Jacob Siegel*

Preface

I spent a good part of my first day as president of the University of Puget Sound simply walking the hundred-acre campus. It was a glorious Pacific Northwest Sunday in July of 1992, and few people were around. I was struck that I had only once before felt the same overwhelming sense of responsibility: when my daughter, Sasha, had been born twenty years earlier. From the moment of her birth, I had never stopped thinking about her. I now recognized that as long as I was president, I would never stop thinking about the college.

A week later, I spent an hour getting my hair cut. The stylist asked if I needed to go back to work after the haircut. I said that I did. She then asked where I worked. I told her. She next asked what I did at the university. When I answered that I was the president, she asked what presidents did. I tried as concisely as I could to tell her. When I finished, she paused for a long time and then asked, "How did you get stuck with *that* job?"

I was right on that July Sunday: I would for the next eleven years as Puget Sound's president think unceasingly about the college. My hairdresser, on the other hand, was wrong because, far from feeling "stuck" with the job, I found it the most satisfying work of my career.

In the ensuing years, as I gained greater experience and also began to work closely with and observe other presidents, either as colleagues in various professional organizations, as a member of accreditation teams, or as a consultant, my answer to the question of what presidents do has become far more complex and nuanced than it was in the summer of 1992.

The Inspiration for This Book

This book, which in great part is intended to answer the question of what good presidents and trustees do, has been inspired not only by my experience at Puget Sound but also by my subsequent work. Specifically, within a year of leaving the university, I began "flunking retirement" and embarked on a new career as a writer and consultant. In the latter role, as president of SRP CONSULTING, I work with boards and presidents on such matters as governance, board development, and board effectiveness; advise colleges and universities on strategic planning; provide guidance to new presidents and their board chairs on a range of matters; and in one extended project, evaluated a sitting president with the board's charge that I seek to help him become more successful. In my role as a search consultant, I have facilitated searches for senior colleges and university administrators (more often than not presidents).

Prior to my presidency, I had been a faculty member, a dean, and then a chief academic officer. In the early 1980s I directed National Endowment for the Humanities programs that funded undergraduate education. I had done occasional consulting, served on accreditation teams, and was a member of a number of higher education boards and commissions.

In 2008 I began writing a series of essays for the online journal *Inside Higher Ed* about matters related to the role and responsibilities of presidents and trustees, and about searches for college and university presidents and vice presidents. I also began speaking at various national meetings about these same topics. The abundant and positive response to these essays and presentations from presidents, aspiring presidents, and trustees assured me that I was right in trying to address these issues in the more expanded way that a book would allow.

Audience

This book is intended for sitting presidents, aspiring presidents, trustees, senior administrators, members of the faculty, and members of presidential search committees, all of whom would, in my judgment, benefit the institutions they serve and enhance their effectiveness by having a clearer understanding of their various roles and responsibilities as well as a fuller understanding of those of the president. The book is also intended to describe the presidential search process, both to demystify it and to provide guidance to all those—search committee members and candidates themselves—who participate in this most important of efforts.

Structure of the Book and Overview

Although logic might suggest that this book begin with a discussion of the presidential search process, I have chosen instead to end it there, in great part because I see the search not as the beginning but rather as one part of a much more complex and important process. To appoint successful presidents, institutions must first become clear about their mission, their aspirations, their strengths, their opportunities and challenges, and presidents, boards, senior administrators, and faculty must all understand their roles, their responsibilities, and their (legitimate) expectations of one another.

In Part One, "Being an Effective President," Chapter One begins with a series of cautionary tales, describing various ways in which presidents fail to provide effective leadership and boards fail to provide necessary support and oversight. At some point in my own career, I began to see that the negatives taught me the most. For example, I learned from several imperial presidents how important it was for me, when I became a president, to be accessible and genuinely engaged in the life of the institution. From an autocratic supervisor, I learned the importance of encouraging my colleagues to be creative. From a micromanaging acting president, I learned the importance of delegating. From a president who sought popularity above all else, I learned that it was more important to be respected than adored. Thus, I have chosen cautionary tales that I hope will inspire my readers to discover better ways of being a president.

Chapter Two sets out to clarify what it is that makes presidents and trustees effective. This chapter also contains a great many specific recommendations for how presidents and boards can work with each other.

Chapter Three focuses on the president's relationship with the various campus constituencies and the local community. Like Chapter Two, it seeks to define how presidents can be effective in relationship to each of these groups and also contains specific recommendations for how they can work with them.

Chapter Four is an even more pivotal chapter than it would have been a decade ago in its premise that successful presidents must be able both to raise money and to manage the institution's financial and human resources if they are to advance the institution's mission with fairness and a commitment to the long-term health of the college or university.

Chapter Five was prompted by a statistic in the ACE report *A National Profile of Chief Academic Officers*: 24 percent of current chief academic officers cite "living in a fishbowl" as one reason why they do not want to become presidents. My goal here is to describe honestly the challenges of being a public figure and offer suggestions for how presidents and their spouses or partners, if they have them, can craft private lives for themselves while living in a public context.

Chapter Six offers suggestions to departing presidents and their boards about how they can (and should) let go and leave gracefully. This chapter talks about some negative situations where presidents, even after voluntarily choosing to retire, attempted to continue to direct their institution. It also provides recommendations for positive and seamless presidential transitions.

Chapter Seven was one of the most enjoyable to write. It describes why so many of my presidential colleagues have found the work enormously satisfying. This chapter, which was informed by stories that a great many former and current presidents shared with me, as well as by my own experience, strives to explain why being a president can bring with it a wonderful sense of accomplishment, much joy, and even fun.

Chapter Eight, the first chapter of Part Two, "Becoming an Effective President," discusses the future of the college presidency, explores the shifting nature of the presidential ranks, and goes into more depth about why declining numbers of chief academic officers want to become presidents and why increasing numbers of colleges and universities are turning to nontraditional candidates. This chapter also offers recommendations for preparing both traditional and nontraditional candidates for the presidency.

The final chapter, Chapter Nine, explains the search process and seeks to advise candidates on how to become competitive. It also makes the argument that the skills required for a successful candidacy are the same as those necessary for a successful presidency.

Ultimately, I wrote this book because I have witnessed again and again both the transforming effect that an excellent college education can have on students and the critical role that presidents can play in inspiring such excellence. At the same time, I am aware of the daunting responsibility that a college presidency brings with it. My hope, therefore, is that this book will help presidents, their boards, and their administrative and faculty colleagues understand what it means to be presidential and that that understanding will enhance presidential leadership and the quality of the educational experience of their students.

Acknowledgments

I am especially grateful to Scott Jashik, *Inside Higher Ed* editor and co-founder, who first encouraged me to write a series of essays on higher education, gave me an ongoing forum for them, and eventually proposed to me that I expand the essays into a book. Scott then suggested to David Brightman, executive editor, Higher and Adult Education at Jossey-Bass, that Jossey-Bass consider publishing the book. I owe David great thanks for his encouragement. I was elated the first time he referred to himself as my editor. I became even more elated as he advised me on ways to improve the book. Aneesa Davenport, assistant editor, was supportive and insightful throughout. Learning that marketing manager Kasi Miller was a Puget Sound graduate who had been a student when I was at Puget Sound was especially meaningful. Marketing assistant Hunter Stark was very helpful. My deepest thanks and highest praise go to Sandra Beris, my copyeditor, who taught me even more than William Strunk, Jr. and E. B. White in their classic *Elements of Style* about making every word count. I also have appreciated the emails from and phone conversations with trustees, presidents, and aspiring presidents who contacted me after reading the *IHE* essays.

I owe thanks to many others, far more than I could name here, but let me begin with personal acknowledgments. Perhaps most importantly, I want to thank my daughter Alexandra (Sasha) Siegel for enriching my life beyond measure. She is always an inspiration to me. My grandsons, Sean and Ryan Siegel, at ages eight and six, thrill me with their love of reading, their fascination with words, and their exuberance for life. My son-in-law, Steven Siegel, simply makes me happy that he is such a loving husband, father, and yes, son-in-law. My late husband Kenneth Pierce was truly my partner during my Puget Sound years. A former corporate CEO, college professor, and trustee, he taught me a great deal and encouraged my sense of the absurd. My wonderful sisters, Linda Resneck Krohn and Brenda Resneck Laughery, our incredible father Elliott Resneck (who throughout our childhood sent us often to dictionaries), and our amazing late mother Dory Resneck with her unconditional love, have always encouraged and supported me. Laird Desmond gave me exemplary help reviewing an early draft of this manuscript, and Dick Turner (former president of Grinnell, which was only one of the many distinguished faculty and administrative positions he held) has over many years been an amazing mentor and an equally stunning friend. Each of these individuals has contributed abundantly to the texture of my life.

My colleagues, current and past, especially Tom Courtice, Rich Ekman, Jamie Ferrare, Bert Sonnenfeld, Tom Staley, Tobie Van der Vorm, and A. Walton Litz, have taught me much and been important friends.

I also want to thank the new presidents with whom I have been privileged to work, the wonderful board and search committee chairs who have taken seriously their responsibility to hire and then become a partner to their college's new presidents, and the Puget Sound community of faculty, staff, students, trustees, donors, parents, and alumni who were willing to go on a journey of change with me.

First among these is my exemplary board chair of ten years Bill Weyerhaeuser, who truly was both my colleague and friend in our effort to make a wonderful college an even better one. Terry Lengfelder, the Puget Sound board vice chair, gave me important guidance at critical moments. Other members of the board, too numerous to name, exemplified what good trustees do.

I am grateful to Karen Goldstein, vice president for finance and administration during my final three years at Puget Sound and my colleague at SRP CONSULTING and Academic Search, for her unwavering friendship, her keen editorial eye, and the pleasure she has brought me by sharing my consulting life. Karen and her Puget Sound vice presidential colleagues, Terry Cooney, Kris Bartanen, and George Mills, demonstrated what talented people, working as a team, could accomplish. Beth Herman, Puget Sound's director of development for nine of the years of my presidency, was a fine fundraising coach.

The following Puget Sound faculty and staff members, among many others, inspired my discussion of presidential collaboration with their colleagues: Bob Albertson, Suzanne Barnett, Kim Bobby, Ava Brock, Ed Cole, Jenell Coughlin, Doug Edwards, Rosa Beth Gibson, Mott Greene, Leon Grunberg, Chong Heyder, Suzanne Holland, Arlene Holt, Chris Ives, Rufus Kennedy, Linda King, Chuck Luce, Paul Loeb, John McGee, Lorraine McNair (whom the students called "Mama Lola"), Maggie Mittuch, Gertrude Moore, Ily Nagy, Faye Nichols, Bev Pierson, Michel Rocchi, Stuart Smithers, Elaine Stefanowicz, Alan Thorndike, Mike Veseth, Keith Ward, Melissa Weinman-Jagosh, Anne Wood, and Lisa Wood.

A host of former and current presidents also were very helpful to me both as I was writing the book and throughout my career, but I am especially grateful to Bruce Alton Leon Botstein, Francesco Cesareo, Constantin (Deno) Curris, Stan Hales, Rock Jones, Jessica Koslow, Marie McDermott, Pat McPherson, Jo Ellen Parker, Bob Parilla, John Pickelman, Steve Poskanzer, Carolynn-Reid Wallace, Kathleen Ross, Stephen Joel Trachtenberg, and Jim Votruba.

Most of all, I want to thank my students, from the time I began teaching as a teaching assistant, next at a community college, and then at wonderful institutions ranging from Ithaca College to Princeton. They have been and continue to be the reason why I do what I do.

About the Author

Susan Resneck Pierce is president emerita of the University of Puget Sound, where she served as president from 1992 to 2003. Under her leadership, Puget Sound entered the ranks of the national liberal arts colleges. As the result of a successful comprehensive campaign and careful use of institutional resources, the endowment grew from $68 million to $213 million; the college completed $85 million of new construction and major renovations; SAT scores increased from 1067 to 1253; and applications for 650 freshman places grew to 4,400 annually. To honor her work at Puget Sound, donors endowed both a chair in humanities and honors and a lecture series in public affairs and the arts in her name. In addition, thanks also to a major donor, the atrium of Puget Sound's new humanities building now carries her name.

From 1990 to 1992 Pierce served as vice president for academic affairs at Lewis & Clark College, and from 1984 to 1990 as dean of the College of Arts and Sciences at the University of Tulsa. As assistant director of the Division of Education Programs at the National Endowment for the Humanities from 1982 to 1984, she directed the three federal programs that supported undergraduate education in the humanities. She also has served as chair of the English Department at Ithaca College and as visiting associate professor at Princeton University. In 2004–05, Susan Pierce served

xxii   About the Author

as president of the Boca Raton Community Hospital Foundation and vice president for the hospital.

The author of *The Moral of the Story* (Columbia University's Teachers College Press, 1982) and co-editor of *Approaches to Teaching Ralph Ellison's Invisible Man* (Modern Language Association of America, 1989), Pierce has written and spoken extensively about American literature and educational issues. She has served on the boards of the Association of American Colleges and Universities (AAC&U) and the American Conference of Academic Deans, on the advisory committee for the AAC&U project on engineering and the liberal arts, on the Council of Presidents of the Association of Governing Boards, and on the Washington Women in Leadership Advisory Committee. She has been active in many civic, cultural, and professional organizations, including the boards of the Seattle Symphony, Hillcrest Medical Center in Tulsa, the Tulsa Chapter of the National Conference of Christians and Jews, and the Tulsa Opera. She cofounded the Access to College program in collaboration with Rudy Crew, then-superintendent of the Tacoma Public Schools. From 1998 to 2002, she served on the National Institute of Alcohol Abuse and Alcoholism Task Force on College Drinking and on the executive committee of the Annapolis Group. She is currently a member of the board for the Centre for the Arts at Mizner Park in Boca Raton and serves both on the steering committee for the Festival of the Arts Boca and as chair of its literature program. She is the recipient of several teaching awards and the Council for Advancement and Support of Education (CASE) District VIII Distinguished Leadership Award for 2003. Susan Pierce is a member of Phi Beta Kappa.

Pierce received her A.B. degree from Wellesley College, her M.A. degree from the University of Chicago, and her Ph.D. from the University of Wisconsin, all in English. She now lives in Boca Raton, Florida, where she is writing and consulting. As president of SRP CONSULTING, she advises colleges and universities on planning, effective board and presidential performance, board development, governance, and fundraising. She has also facilitated presidential and senior administrative searches for colleges and universities.

On Being Presidential

Part I

Being an Effective President

1

Some Cautionary Tales

I have been privileged throughout my career to work with and learn from some exemplary presidents who, among other things, created and executed data-informed, mission-based, and financially sound strategic plans; were committed to teaching and learning; fostered teamwork; encouraged creativity; and communicated effectively both to internal and external audiences, thereby inspiring commitment from both groups. I have been equally privileged to work with exceptional trustees who provided their presidents with support and counsel, saw themselves as the president's strategic partner, and gave generously of their time, their talent, and their resources to the institutions they served. I have also worked with faculty leaders who, in addition to being exemplary teachers and sometimes admirable scholars, thought institutionally and collaborated with the administration to advance the college or university.

At the same time, I have been saddened and dismayed by the number of colleges and universities that have been damaged by ineffective presidents or indifferent or incompetent boards. Specifically, far too many colleges and universities—despite their talented faculty and promising students, and despite well-meaning presidents and trustees—have, in my judgment, suffered from a significant and sometimes devastating failure of presidential leadership and trustee oversight. As a result, many of these institutions have encountered serious financial problems, declining enrollments, and tarnished reputations.

Leo Tolstoy began *Anna Karenina* by observing, "Happy families are all alike; every unhappy family is unhappy in its own way." And so it is with presidents and boards. Despite the diversity of the institutions they serve, successful presidents and effective boards exhibit common behaviors, whereas unsuccessful ones are unsuccessful in a variety of different ways. Thus, with apologies for beginning with the negatives, let me offer some cautionary tales before turning in the next chapters to how presidents, trustees, senior administrators, and faculty leaders can avoid making these mistakes, and even more importantly, how they can be highly effective instead.

Presidential Missteps

The world of higher education is replete with stories of presidents who have floundered, often in their first several years. (Fortunately, there are many more examples of presidents who succeed in the first year and beyond, but as John Milton demonstrated so brilliantly in *Paradise Lost*, it is the character who suffers a fall that often is the more compelling.) In many of these instances, the presidents used poor judgment, acting without first consulting their boards, thereby losing the confidence of their trustees and often losing their presidencies. In only a few cases did the presidents act out of anything other than the best of motives, but their unilateral decision making had serious if not disastrous consequences for their institutions.

In other examples, well-meaning and committed trustees deferred too much to presidents whom they judged to be successful, failing to ask questions, request important data, require effective strategic plans, insist on balanced budgets, and hold presidents accountable. These trustees often defined their fiduciary responsibility quite narrowly to financial matters, serving diligently on the finance, facilities, audit, and investment committees but considering each of those functions as separate from the institutional mission or strategic priorities. The presidents in each of these examples did not educate their boards about institutional problems, challenges, and opportunities or about the national landscape of higher education. The trustees, many of whom were successful corporate executives, accepted behaviors from the administration that they would not tolerate in their own companies.

On campuses, there is often a lack of understanding of what the president does (and should do) beyond raising money and about the larger issues facing the institution, issues that the president grapples with daily. This lack of understanding tends to be accompanied by confusion about the appropriate role and responsibilities not only of the faculty but also of the president and the trustees. On some campuses, there is also a tradition of faculty opposition to the administration, regardless of the issue. I have witnessed myriad examples where the faculty and the administration and sometimes the faculty and the board find themselves at odds over governance. The resulting conflict often paralyzes institutions and in some instances leads to a failed presidency.

Many of the specific examples I cite have been covered in the press. The others I've either learned about from friends and colleagues or observed firsthand as a member of an accreditation team or the administration, or as a consultant. In all instances, I have tried to disguise the identities of the institutions and the presidents—sometimes but not always changing the gender of the individuals or the nature of the institution. Taken as a whole, these examples illustrate the need for more effective presidential leadership, more effective board oversight, and a better understanding on the part of boards and campuses of what presidents do.

Judgment

Prominent among the presidents who alienated their campuses and lost the confidence of their boards are those who have spent excessive and sometimes even exorbitant sums on renovating the president's house prior to or immediately after arriving on campus, thereby worrying the board and alienating the campus. One such president of a financially strapped college overspent the budget for the president's house renovation by 50 percent and then defended himself by arguing illogically that since he would be living there, it would have been a "conflict of interest" for him to have over-seen the renovation budget. A second president similarly justified the overspending by pleading that the board had approved some of the renovations and that he had not been involved in all the spending decisions. A third president spent more than $1 million renovating what the campus thought was an already-lovely resi-dence at a time when the college was cutting departmental budgets and constraining salaries. Each of these individuals was ultimately terminated.

Other presidents have created problems for themselves by an-nouncing plans to change their institution in ways that the current board, faculty, staff, students, or alumni found disparaging. In one widely publicized incident, a new president announced his plan to upgrade the quality of the students, implicitly denigrating the university's alumni by asserting that without such an improvement, the university would not be able to transform its students into high achievers but rather would simply turn "mush into mush." Another began his tenure by announcing that the college, which histori-cally had attracted students because of its emphasis on teaching and which had a minimal endowment and limited resources for faculty development, would base all future tenure and promotion decisions on publication in prestigious journals and presses. An-other new president at a top-tier institution squandered his hon-eymoon period by unceremoniously firing longtime staff members, many of whom had the respect of the board and the affection of the faculty. Then there was the first-semester president who an-nounced his plan to downgrade athletics and eliminate the Greek system, somehow overlooking the fact that many of his trustees had themselves been student-athletes and members of fraternities and sororities.

Communication

In contrast, some presidents overstate their institution's successes. I've known several cases where sitting presidents have persuaded their boards that their institution is poised for national prominence because of what they characterize as the college's unique commitment to such commonplace initiatives as civic engagement, service learning, global education, social justice, student-faculty research, and close relationships among and between students, faculty, and staff. They represent their institution as being a pathfinder and a national leader in one or more of these areas. In one such instance, it took a presidential candidate to encourage the trustees to review the websites of the university's peer institutions—all laying claim to the same initiatives and some actually doing a great deal more than this college was. In this case, the trustees came to understand that what the college was doing was indeed praiseworthy but just was not unique or even distinctive and certainly would not bring it the prominence that the retiring president had promised.

Other presidents have made decisions that may well have had merit but angered their trustees because they neglected to consult or communicate with them about the decisions. In two such cases, influential trustees were angered when they learned about a significant presidential decision not from the president but in the press. By ignoring the principle that presidents should never surprise their boards with bad news, these presidents lost the confidence of their trustees and ultimately their presidencies.

There are also presidents who have damaged their presidency by viewing the faculty as their adversaries. For example, one former president became so enraged at his faculty colleagues that he stormed out of a faculty meeting, telling them as he slammed the door behind him, "You're incorrigible. You're all children." Another equally unhappy president resigned, telling his board that the faculty "wouldn't let him do anything" and that they needed to get the faculty under control. The faculty members at these institutions were equally unhappy and felt disenfranchised.

Management Style

Some presidents fail to advance their institutions because of their management style. Some are motivated by a desire for popularity rather than respect. Some refuse to draw the wrath of the faculty by recommending to the board that it deny tenure or promotion to a faculty member. For example, a relatively new president announced to the faculty that he would deny tenure to any candidate that he or they deemed questionable. He privately directed the provost to be "tough." Most of those considered for tenure that year had, in the provost's judgment, clearly earned it. In two cases, however, the departments had been split (something unusual at this small college, where the faculty historically endorsed all candidates for tenure) and the elected faculty tenure and promotion committees had been split as well. The provost, having taken seriously the president's directive that she be "tough," recommended against tenure for both. Her recommendation was greeted with anger on the part of the candidates' friends and supporters. In the face of intense lobbying, the president overruled her. The provost, feeling undercut, went on the market, and in what seemed a moment of poetic justice, became president of a competitor college.

Other presidents, seeking popularity, approve most requests for resources without regard to mission or finances. One such individual, in a year when there was an enrollment shortfall and debt already close to the size of the endowment, nevertheless borrowed several million dollars and overspent the operating budget by $2 million. He was simply unwilling to say no to any new idea. Another president, in the face of significant budget deficits, announced that he did not want the budget to inhibit planning. In so doing, he inadvertently gave the message that the funds would be there for every good idea. In both cases, there ultimately was huge campus disappointment and disillusionment. Yet other presidents have persuaded their boards to approve an increase in the size of the student body with the intent of gaining more tuition and room and board revenue, only to learn that the additional students did not materialize.

There are also some presidents who are simply afraid to make decisions. Some prefer ongoing conversation about alternatives. Some simply prefer planning to action. Their paralysis inevitably paralyzes those who report to them because they cannot move forward without presidential approval. One president was unable to recommend a set of fundraising priorities to the board—despite campus consensus that the greatest needs were additional financial aid endowment, new faculty positions, a new library, and a new academic building—delaying the beginning of the campaign by at least a year.

There are also many examples of micromanaging presidents whose insistence on being involved in all decisions inevitably stifles creativity and initiative. My favorite example of micromanagement is this: the president who insisted on reviewing and approving the food served for all catered events on campus. He worried about the menu, even down to the quality of the salads being served at luncheons.

Some micromanaging presidents foster competition rather than collaboration among their senior staff. These presidents tend to tolerate, if not encourage, silos rather than teamwork. They work in a spoke-and-hub way, with they themselves being the hub. This model requires each of the president's direct reports to work directly with him or her, thereby dividing the senior staff. In one memorable instance, a senior administrator told me that no one at her institution would willingly share information. Rather, she said, if required to do so, people would "throw the information over the transom" of the door of those with whom they were sharing. They would, however, refuse to interpret or analyze that information.

Planning

Presidents need to be wary of developing strategic plans that are neither strategic nor plans but rather constituency-driven wish lists. Such documents always seem to have titles that envision a bright future for the institution. Unhappily, these plans generally do not derive from the institutional mission, establish strategic priorities, tie the identified hopes and dreams to budgets (current and future), offer time lines, assign responsibility for actions, hold people accountable for results, or suggest methods of assessment. Nor do they differentiate between the strategic and the tactical.

The strategic planning document developed at one regional university is a case in point. This nearly forty-page list of desired initiatives and programs was to be the institution's blueprint for the future. The problem: everything in the plan was something that someone or some group wanted, but there was no effort to prioritize the items or differentiate between institutional imperatives and things that would simply be nice to do if the college someday secured the resources to do them. By blurring the strategic and the tactical and giving equal weight to all goals, the plan suggested that improving the quality of the student body and buying equipment for the art department were, like all goals, of equivalent value. Nor did the document identify the costs (much less the benefits) of each item noted, the time frame in which things were to happen, the method of assessment, or the people charged with making each one happen. Moreover, the president had instructed the planning teams not to worry about resources but rather to describe the university of their dreams in twenty years.

There was a similar situation at a small private college where the president announced that the budget would not drive planning but that planning would drive budget. He was right, of course, but his message was heard very differently from what he intended. What the campus and the CFO heard was that the college should dream big and worry about resources later. As a result, neither the college's operating budget nor its five-year financial plan allocated funds for the strategic initiatives that the president and board had approved. Over time, the faculty felt betrayed that the new faculty lines they had been promised to mount the new core curriculum were not materializing.

Then there are those presidents who plan in a piecemeal fashion. One announced that the academic vice president and faculty needed first to develop an academic strategic plan and, only when that was approved, would the campus turn to the resource question and planning in other areas. The result: the campus spent a good deal of time planning in the abstract but eventually learned that they lacked the resources to implement the plan and that a number of their goals were mutually contradictory.

Other institutions have found themselves in trouble because their strategic plans and three- to five-year financial plans were based on overly optimistic assumptions. Rather than building these budgets conservatively—on numbers they were confident they could achieve, for example—some institutions created long-term problems for themselves by predicating their planning on hoped-for increases in such revenue lines as enrollment, the annual fund, and income from the endowment. Some have done so even when their institutions had experienced declining numbers in one or more of these areas in recent years. When the anticipated revenues did not materialize, these colleges and universities have faced budgetary shortfalls, sometimes of a significant magnitude.

Finally, there are those situations when the presidents did not monitor or perhaps even understand the budget, simply accepting the word of their CFO that everything was fine. For example, the financial vice president of a college suffering declining enrollments repeatedly reassured his financially naive president that he should not worry that they had just enrolled one hundred fewer freshmen than budgeted because, the CFO insisted, the budget was based on a three-year rolling average. It took a new provost to explain to the president that although it made sense to calculate the endowment payout based on a three-year rolling average, a hundred-student shortfall at an institution that charged $40,000 per year for tuition and room and board was an immediate and very serious financial problem. She also explained that this shortfall would affect total enrollment for the next four years. The president put the provost in charge of the budget, including making the necessary cuts.

The retiring president and the financial vice president of another troubled institution had persuaded the board that the institution was not ready for a strategic plan that included a realistic long-term financial plan and fiscal discipline. This is an interesting case study because both the president and the CFO understood that to balance the college budget, the university—like many others—was going to need to do some combination of the following: reduce staff, freeze salaries and all hiring, decrease department budgets, put capital projects on hold, and reduce benefits, including contributions to retirement funds. Concerned about the president's popularity, however, neither wanted to make the hard choices. Instead, they persuaded the board to make another bad decision: to fund the deficit by increasing the draw on the endowment, which had decreased significantly because of the economic downturn, to more than 9 percent. This decision, which harmed the institution's long-term economic viability, also postponed the problem by only one year. The next president's first months were spent eliminating faculty and staff positions and reducing spending across the institution.

Visibility

Presidents who refuse to socialize with the campus community create other problems for themselves. They appear remote and uninterested. Here are a few of my favorite stories about such presidents:

- When an out-of-touch president was invited to a dinner party at the home of a department chair, he first responded by telling the chair that he was thrilled with her invitation because this was the first time he had ever been invited to a faculty member's home. Unfortunately, he then provided the following condition to his accepting: his hostess must not invite other faculty members to the dinner.

- A long-term president drove from his on-campus home to his office, scurried into the building, and left only at the end of the day to drive home. When he attended campus events, he came late, sat in the back, and left early. The student government leaders joked that if he showed up at one of their meetings, no one would know who he was.

- Four now-former presidents spent all their on-campus time in their offices, all located on the top floor of a building seldom frequented by students and faculty. Each of these presidents refused to eat in the student dining hall. One, however, went so far as to close the faculty-staff dining room in the student center and in its place create a president's dining room, complete with an extravagant chandelier and expensive china. His only guests were trustees, potential donors, and visitors to the campus. The campus referred to him as an "imperial president." He enjoyed no support.

- Yet another president, who had been in office for more than twenty years, similarly stayed in his office when he was on campus. He became outraged when, on his way to a reception for donors in the rare book room, he was denied entrance to the library because he did not have a campus ID and the staff member at the door did not recognize him. His solution was not to become more visible on campus; instead, he distributed his 9 by 12 inch photograph to every office on campus.

Presidents Who Deceive Their Boards

Perhaps the most serious problems occur when presidents deliberately mislead their boards. In several such cases, the presidents were so averse to delivering bad news that they held off sharing problems with the trustees until they had no choice but to do so. The result: they not only undermined their relationship with their trustees—and by extension, their institution—but failed to benefit from the advice that their trustees might have given them.

- One admired president established a practice of reporting inflated SAT scores to *US News and World Report.* Several of his senior staff members were involved in the deception. His successor had the unhappy task of disclosing the dishonest reporting to the board. For what she considered to be the health of the institution, the new president chose not to share the information that the numbers had been inflated with the campus. Unfortunately, she had to preside over the decline in ratings that accompanied the now-honest reporting.

- The president of an institution that had done a great deal of borrowing, without consulting with his board, loaned an alumnus $10 million on the promise of a 12 percent return in six months. The story illustrates the cliché that "if it seems to be too good to be true, it is too good to be true." At the end of the six months, the company declared bankruptcy. Eventually, the story hit the papers, and the president resigned.

- The president of an NCAA Division I university and his financial vice president deceived the board about the millions of dollars the athletic program was losing annually by hiding the salaries of the coaches in the budgets of academic departments. The departments and the academic dean did not know this was happening because the budget reports they received did not include the coaches. Shortly after discovering this deception, the dean quietly chose to leave the institution. The president named a crony to the deanship.

As troubling as these examples are, the most egregious failures of presidential responsibility have resulted when presidents created a culture of fear and control on their campuses in order to manipulate their boards.

In one case, a second-term president warned the members of his cabinet that if they told the board the truth about certain situations or in any way did not enthusiastically support him, he would immediately fire them. These vice presidents kept their own counsel for several years. For example, they did not tell the trustees that they were to a person opposed to a major and expensive presidential initiative that led to significant presidential travel overseas. Ultimately, they shared their concerns with a consultant who had been hired to facilitate a trustee retreat. The consultant shared this information with the board leadership, who immediately investigated the charges and began a search for a new president.

Another president similarly demanded that the vice presidents join him in hiding information from the trustees, in this case the institution's unusually high attrition rate and the fact that, in order to balance its budget, the university was admitting but not reporting large numbers of transfers. The administration routinely gave presentations to the board about programs they said the university was offering successfully. These programs did not exist. An accreditation team discovered the dishonesty and reported it to the board, which immediately asked for the president's resignation.

The Importance of Board Oversight

A popular president, credited with enhancing the quality of the university he led and significantly increasing the size of its enrollments and its endowment, was unexpectedly asked to resign because of financial irregularities. As a press release from the institution explained, the institution was awarding scholarships over the amount allocated in the budget, and in some cases, greater than that permitted by federal guidelines. Then, to cover the costs of this additional financial aid but without board knowledge or approval, the university borrowed money. Only after the fact did the board chair recognize that the board, in part because it had more than sixty members serving on twelve committees, had not fulfilled its fiduciary responsibilities.

This board was not alone in failing to provide appropriate oversight:

- The trustees of a midsize regional college were proud of their balanced budgets. Mistakenly assuming that benchmarking was taking place, they accepted the president's assertions that all decisions tied in any way to operations were under his purview. They did not ask to see comparative data. Moreover, this board came together only twice a year for two-hour meetings during which the president regaled them with glowing reports of the college's successes. When the president retired, the board and the campus celebrated his many achievements. The next president found herself burdened with the task of telling them that the college's tuition discount had grown to more than

50 percent, its net tuition revenue was inadequate, and the campus had significant deferred maintenance.

- The board of a small and once-thriving college had for a number of years feared that the institution was barely viable. Its reputation was in tatters, its enrollment under budget, and many of its buildings visibly crumbling. A new president, who, by partnering with the local community, had implemented some revenue-producing programs, was widely viewed as the campus savior. Thus, the board didn't question his assertion that the college was unique—with no other comparable schools in the country—and rubber-stamped his recommendations because, as one trustee put it, "The recommendations just felt right." Riding the wave of reputed success, this president moved on to a more affluent university. Only then did the board learn that the college was still very much on the edge, having spent down much of its endowment principle to fund programs that were neither cost-effective nor central to its mission.

- The board of a comprehensive regional university assured presidential candidates that the campus had absolutely no deferred maintenance. The longtime chair of the finance and facilities committee was especially proud that this modestly endowed university was, in his judgment, unique because of its fulsome investment in the physical plant. The outgoing president and the financial vice president told candidates the same story. On her first day in office, the new president asked the director of facilities to give her a tour of the campus, pointing out places needing maintenance. Learning that the sum for such repairs came to more than $200 million, she asked the financial vice president for an explanation. His response: since he and the previous president had decided they were never going to spend money on maintenance, it hadn't been deferred. When the president told the board about the new reality, she suggested that the phrase used should actually have been "denied maintenance." With no small measure of embarrassment, the finance and facilities committee members admitted that they had never asked for an audit of campus buildings and none of them had toured faculty offices, classrooms, or residence halls, all of which screamed out for renovation.

- Finally, the board of an elite university believed that its longtime and widely praised president had earned the right to focus on whatever he wished. He had, after all, in his first decade raised lots of money, transformed the campus, and improved the quality of the students and faculty. Thus, the board was accepting when he turned his attention away from the campus and became a player in the local community, the state capital, and Washington, DC. They were unaware that the faculty and senior staff had begun to talk about mission drift. They did not know that the loyal financial vice president lost sleep worrying about a dramatic increase in the financial aid discount, the growing list of deferred maintenance and infrastructure problems, and the amount of resources being deflected from campus priorities to the president's pet projects. The 2008 economic downturn made it clear to the president that cuts would need to be made. But rather than doing unpopular things, and wishing to preserve his legacy as a builder, he gave notice. His successor was handed the list of concerns.

Endowment Payout and Borrowing

As in the preceding case, the trustees on a number of campuses have in the last decade naively assumed that their institution's endowment would continue to produce handsome returns. They therefore readily authorized spending down the quasi-endowment in order to fund presidential recommendations. Many other colleges failed to consider the long-term impact on the institution of not adhering to a reasonable endowment payout—usually 4 to 5 percent—and not requiring a balanced budget. I know of several institutions that, having enjoyed a handsome return on their endowment, year after year authorized payouts ranging from 8 to 12 percent. Today, the operating budgets of these institutions are suffering for two reasons. First, their endowments did not grow during the years when the market was climbing and so they created no cushion for themselves for difficult financial times. Second, when their endowment dropped in value in 2008, they not only had to contend with reduced principle but also understood that they could no longer continue such large payouts. In other words, they suddenly were able to allocate to the operating budget only 4 to 6 percent of a substantially smaller endowment.

Other boards, including those of some of the most prestigious colleges and universities in the country, approved building projects to be funded by borrowing rather than through fundraising or institutional reserves. Over time, this approach had a devastating impact on their endowments and operating budgets. *Liquidity and Credit Risk at Endowed U.S. Universities and Not-for-Profits*, a June 14, 2010 report put out by Moody's, describes the negative consequences of what has become an increasing reliance across higher education and other not-for-profits on borrowing, often with variable rate debt, creating significant liquidity problems for these institutions.

Jack Stripling, writing for *Inside Higher Ed* in a June 16, 2010 piece, "Moody's Probes Colleges on Cash," summarized the report this way:

> The report notes, for instance, that college leaders were often convinced impressive investment returns would cover operations, and they were inclined to borrow money to fund capital projects, rather than tap endowment funds that were making money in real estate, private equity, hedge funds and other strategies.

To finance capital projects, colleges increasingly hoped to lower borrowing costs by issuing variable rate debt. While that seemed like a good idea at the time, issuing variable rather than fixed rate debt later subjected colleges to volatile interest rates when the credit markets contracted. As debt financing demands grew, and investment dollars were increasingly tied up in long-term instruments, problems emerged for many colleges—as evidenced by the need to borrow more money or tighten belts just to pay the bills. The problems were particularly pronounced at large endowment institutions, which were heavily reliant on investment returns to fund operations and also had significant illiquid investments.

The reality is that colleges can no longer assume—as they did for many years—that their endowments will continue to grow, generating ever-greater revenue for their operating budgets. They also can no longer predicate their future budgets based on past performance because of new uncertainties about enrollment. Some private colleges, for instance, are suffering from decreased enrollment because students who would previously have chosen them have instead enrolled at public institutions or community colleges. Ironically, many public institutions have found these increased numbers a problem, because many state legislatures have significantly reduced funding for higher education.

The Importance of Clear Expectations

Many of these cases suggest that if the presidents had simply used common sense and the boards had been more attentive to what was happening on campus, the institutions would have avoided significant problems. I think this is true, but I also have to believe that the great majority of these unhappy situations could have been avoided if—at the time of the presidential appointment—the trustees and president had come to an understanding about how they would work together, who was responsible for what, what sort of information the board wanted to review routinely, and what sort of actions would require board approval.

Such situations also could have been avoided if both the president and the board had been clear about the board's expectations for what constitutes a strategic plan. Instead, as mentioned earlier and discussed in more depth in the next chapter, far too many presidents lead processes that produce nothing more than wish lists, and far too many boards enthusiastically endorse the documents that emerge from such processes.

Most presidents do want to do the right thing for the colleges and universities they serve, and most trustees are eager to make a difference in the institutions on whose boards they sit. But many presidents have no one to turn to for guidance, and many trustees have not served on other college or university boards and so simply assume that the way that this board functions is how it's done. The next chapters will seek to answer the question of what presidents and trustees need to do to be effective.

2

The President and the Board

College and university trustees and presidents share an important responsibility. Although they do so in different ways, all are entrusted with the health and integrity—financial, academic, and institutional—of the institutions they serve. They are partners in the noble enterprise of educating the next generation of citizens. They are inextricably intertwined because presidents recommend the institutional mission, priorities, policies, and budget to the board, which has the ultimate responsibility in each of these areas. In healthy institutions, boards and presidents agree about the mission of the institution and the president's vision for realizing and advancing it.

Boards and presidents are bound together in one other critical way: it is the boards that hire, and in unfortunate circumstances, fire, presidents. In the best of all worlds, the board elects a president who will successfully be the chief executive officer of the college, who will serve effectively as an ex officio member of the board of trustees, and who—along with his or her senior staff—will implement college policies and manage the college. In less happy circumstances, trustees find themselves second-guessing the president, rejecting the president's recommendations, and sometimes micromanaging the institution. When this happens, the trustees almost certainly need to search for a new president.

There are, to be sure, some profound differences between the boards of private institutions and those of public institutions. At the same time, presidents and boards in all sectors have comparable responsibilities. This chapter will briefly describe the differences between these boards, endeavor to define the role of the president and the vast array of presidential responsibilities, and finally, describe the board's important role and responsibilities.

Differences Between Public and Private Boards

Most boards of private institutions are self-perpetuating. Many if not all of their members are alumni. The president plays a significant role in identifying and cultivating new board members. The board can, at its own discretion, go into closed session with only the trustees and the president, or it can go into executive session, meeting without the president. Board members can participate in retreats from which guests are excluded. In short, private college boards are not governed by sunshine laws or state policies.

In contrast, the board members—often called regents—of many public universities are appointed by an elected official, often the governor. Some boards contain a mixture of those appointed by an elected official and those selected by the institution. When an elected official has appointing authority, presidents or chancellors often can recommend future board members but may not have any influence over the outcome. It is common for elected officials to appoint people who share their political views or have made financial contributions to them or their party even though their appointees have no connection to the institution or little knowledge about higher education.

One extremely successful president of a public university explained that the positive aspect of working with trustees in the latter category was being able to educate them about the university's needs and higher education generally. She found these "teachable moments" extremely satisfying. In contrast, she despaired of board members and legislators who were serving only for personal gain or to reward friends, for instance, by securing honorary degrees for them. As she put it, "It is very difficult when your 'boss' (whether a board member or legislator) is doing something either just plain stupid or perhaps unethical, and you can't do anything about it. Well, at least, you have to be very careful about what you do, often taking very circuitous routes."

A second public university president, in a state where all board members are appointed by the governor, recognized after several years that all of those who had been serving when he was hired had been replaced. Adding to his anxiety was the recognition that the first group of board members had been appointed by a governor who was a strong advocate for public higher education, whereas the new board members had been selected by a new governor determined to cut funding.

Public boards also can have very different responsibilities. Some are responsible for all public institutions in the state. Others focus on one sector of public institutions, such as community colleges. Yet others serve as the board for several campuses.

In their 1991 book for the ACE Macmillan Series on Higher Education, *The Effective Board of Trustees*, Richard P. Chait, Thomas P. Holland, and Barbara E. Taylor make further distinctions between the boards of public and private institutions:

> We believe that trustees of public college boards, as a rule, have less consensus than their peers at independent colleges about the board's fundamental role. Whatever their philosophical or educational differences, trustees of private colleges almost invariably perceive the board's essential role as being the guardian of the institution's long-term welfare. We have the impression from news reports and from workshops and conversations with many trustees of public institutions that they, in contrast, often view themselves as public watchdogs,

> constituency representatives or emissaries of partisan po-
> litical interests. In addition, many public boards cannot,
> as a matter of state statute, meet privately, in whole or
> in part, or conduct a closed and confidential retreat to
> reflect freely and to speak bluntly about the board's per-
> formance. Others are reluctant, in any case, to invest
> public funds for this purpose. [p. 7]

Many public university presidents feel hindered by sunshine laws. In Florida, for instance, if two members of the same board or a board member and the president, either formally or casually, discuss any matter that might conceivably come before the board for action, their being together constitutes a public meeting. Even if their conversation took place while they were driving together to a board meeting, they would have needed to advertise their con-versation before getting together and make it open to the public, including the press. The sunshine law, while excluding delibera-tions about individual personal matters, applies to interviews that a search committee might have with a consultant, interviews with presidential candidates, and board retreats. As a result, presidents cannot share confidentially with their board their concerns or their assessment of some aspect or another of their campus community.

Presidents of public institutions also have the responsibility of working with the legislature and other elected officials. Here too the nature of their role may vary. Some legislatures, like those in Texas and Wisconsin, are located only blocks from the flagship university in their state. A former president at one of these univer-sities reported that legislators routinely read the student newspaper and called him with questions. He also noted that faculty members often went to legislators with their concerns. Other legislatures are located in cities some distance from the university, and so their members tend not to be as involved in the life of the university.

The president of a public university with extensive and effective experience working with the state legislature offers new presidents, particularly those of public campuses, some wise and interesting advice:

> Regarding legislators, my advice is simple and straightforward: Place yourself in their world. Don't expect them to place themselves in yours. This involves understanding the world of the legislator and governor sufficiently to align your own agenda with their priorities. Those presidents whom I've known as very effective in the legislative arena understand that, for the public policymakers, higher education is a means to a broader set of public (and possibly constituent) purposes, not an end in itself.
>
> When I sit down with a policymaker, I don't talk "inside baseball." Rather, I describe what we're doing for inter-generational mobility, economic growth, P–12 enhancement, health care access, and a host of other priorities that are particularly important to the policymaker. This means that I begin by asking policymakers about what challenges their constituents confront and then map our campus on those challenges.
>
> One final suggestion for [all presidents who work with legislatures]: Don't waste valuable time with policymakers whining about the difficulties of the current budget environment and how things on your campus are going to hell in a handbasket because of budget cuts. They've heard it all before and, frankly, they're tired of it. Talk vision. Focus on what you *can* do to advance an important public agenda. Talk about the contribution that your campus *can* make to achieving a bright future for all. Certainly, presidents must acknowledge the impact of budget cuts, but legislators are more likely to get excited about a president who is focused on opportunities than they are on a president who is in handwringing mode.

Another president of a regional public campus, after stressing the importance of establishing personal relationships with legislators and finding common ground with them, described the importance of being nonpartisan and maintaining integrity:

> It's essential to get to know your representatives personally and to establish a high level of trust and candor with them. While there will inevitably be some disagreements, I always found it helpful to seek whatever common ground I could find on issues (even issues somewhat removed from higher education). I was careful to remain a registered "independent" so as not to be drawn into partisan disputes, and I had to "draw some lines" to reflect and ensure institutional integrity, such as never admitting students or filling jobs based on political considerations. But I found that the legislators with whom I worked respected these boundaries and that they also respected me for being forthright with them. When disputes occurred, I would voice my criticism and disappointments in private, never "calling out" the elected leaders by name. Embarrassing them in public would have been counterproductive.

The growing decline over the last decades in state funding for public universities has led a number of these institutions to seek more autonomy and to be freed from what they consider to be burdensome regulations and control. For example, as Jack Stripling reports in a March 13, 2011 piece in the *Chronicle of Higher Education* titled "Flagships Just Want to Be Alone," in 2005 the University of Virginia, the College of William and Mary, and Virginia Tech entered into "restructuring agreements" with the state of Virginia. The same piece notes that state funding from 2003 to 2008 declined significantly for some flagship universities, with the University of Colorado at Boulder seeing an 86 percent decline in state appropriations for students, the University of Rhode Island 44 percent, and Pennsylvania State University 42 percent. The state of Oregon provided "just 10 percent of the university's total revenues in the 2009 fiscal year" (p. A4).

The President's Role and Responsibilities

Until well into the twentieth century, the primary role of college and university presidents was to be the moral and sometimes spiritual leaders of their campuses, devoting most of their time to the faculty, students, staff, trustees, and alumni. A few notable presidents like Derek Bok of Harvard, Theodore Hesburgh of Notre Dame, and Clark Kerr of the University of California at Berkeley, also assumed the role of public intellectual, speaking and writing about matters related to higher education.

Although the expectation remains, particularly on small campuses, that the president will be "present" on campus, participating in and often presiding over campus events and attending plays, concerts, athletic events, and lectures, trustees and at least some members of the campus community increasingly want their president to be effective externally as well. They want him or her to be a successful fundraiser, a persuasive and even eloquent public spokesperson (often on a national level), and someone able to provide leadership in positioning the institution.

Boards also seek individuals who will run the institution effectively, have experience with budgets, and allocate and reallocate resources in ways that are creative, fair, and mission-driven. They want their president to understand (and capitalize on) the interplay between the financial aid discount and net tuition revenue, to create inclusive processes, and to communicate effectively with the campus. Many trustees, particularly of tuition-dependent institutions, also want a president who can generate new revenue streams.

Boards further seek presidents who, after consultation with and in some instances actions by various campus groups, regularly inform, educate, and recommend to the board such important matters as mission, vision, strategic imperatives and priorities, fundraising goals, the addition or elimination of programs, the budget, tenure and promotion, appointments of senior staff, and institutional policies.

Understandably, trustees also want frequent and honest presidential communication with the board. A trustee on a presidential search committee explained that "this time, the board would like a president who will tell us when he or she has made a mistake." He contrasted this type of president with those he had worked with previously, who, he said, only shared their successes.

In addition, presidents need to be able to respond to an array of forces beyond their control. For example, because most private colleges and increasing numbers of public institutions are tuition-dependent, their financial stability requires that they enroll a sufficient combination of the budgeted number of first-year students, transfers, and returning students even though the number of students enrolled is influenced by such external factors as the economy and the levels of financial aid that competitor institutions offer. As noted earlier, public institutions for their part are deeply affected by the decline in state money allocated to them.

Most presidents learn pretty quickly that their job in great part is to be interrupted. Even presidents who carefully plan how they will use their time are often pulled away from their intended schedule in order to respond, for example, to unexpected requests, unanticipated needs for a decision, or public relations crises. Such crises may be the result of unanticipated and destructive behavior on the part of a member of the campus community, such as students who are destructive to property, other people, or themselves; faculty, staff, and students who sexually or otherwise harass others; senior administrators or faculty members who plagiarize speeches or papers; outspoken members of the campus community who have alienated key supporters; and trustees who try to exert inappropriate influence.

Given the array of responsibilities and events beyond their control, it is critical that presidents think and act both strategically and tactically, sometimes in relation to the same issue and often at the same time. On the one hand, they need to provide thoughtful, informed, nimble, and creative leadership to enable the institution to fulfill its mission and to realize its aspirations. On the other hand, they need to resist becoming captive to the tyranny of the immediate even as they attend to the immediate and seek to ensure that the institution runs smoothly.

Presidential responsibilities also sometimes are in conflict with one another. For instance, although presidents do need to take the time to learn as much as they can, often by listening to others, about matters at hand so that they can make good decisions, they also need to make decisions in a timely fashion. The challenge for them is to know what they need to learn, to whom they need to listen, how much knowledge and understanding is enough, and what "timely" means. This is no small matter because presidents on a typical day are confronted with a great many decisions both large and small. Indeed, failing to act can become as damaging to the college as making a wrong decision.

The good news is that effective presidents generally are quick studies who begin the process of understanding the institution they now serve the moment they decide to become a candidate. Certainly, most of those who advance to the semi-finalist stage in the search process have already learned a great deal about the institution, reading at least the following:

- All pertinent financial information including the operating budget, the audited financial statement, the long-range financial plan, debt and the debt service, the size of the endowment, and the policy governing the endowment payout

- All strategic plans

- The master plan

- All accreditation self-studies and reports from accrediting agencies

- Information about admissions, retention, graduation rates, and the financial aid discount

- Information about fundraising, including gift totals and alumni participation in the annual fund

- A description of the curriculum

- Information about the co-curriculum, including athletics

- All annual reports

- The current president's speeches and publications

- Minutes of board meetings

- Governance documents, including the board's bylaws

Even as I agree with Judith Block McLaughlin in her book *Leadership Transitions: The New College President*, published in 1996 by Jossey-Bass, that there is a greater risk for new presidents who move too quickly than for presidents who are overly cautious, I disagree with those who interpret this to mean that new presidents should not take significant actions during this first year. For example, I differ with Patrick H. Sanaghan, Larry Goldstein, and Kathleen D. Gavel, who, in their book *Presidential Transitions*, published as part of the ACE/Praeger Series on Higher Education in 2008, argue that new presidents should "not try to move too fast or seek to accomplish too much in their first year. Intelligent change takes time" (p. 25). The reality today is that the significant issues that most presidents need to address require carefully conceived and often immediate actions, but immediate actions nevertheless. As one vice president on a campus that was faced with enroll-ment and financial challenges in the midst of a strategic plan-ning process aptly put it, "We have to cross the bridge even as we build it."

The question for presidents of course is how to find the right balance between taking the time to learn about the campus and acting expeditiously. Here, it is critical that they choose carefully the areas in which they will act and focus only on decisions and actions that have genuine priority. They need to understand poten-tial criticism of their decision or action and be able to address that criticism. They need to try to be as inclusive in implementing the decision or carrying out the action as possible. They also need to be assured of board support before they act. For example, the incom-ing president of a college that was facing a decline in new students enrolling and in retention immediately talked with the board and the faculty about his wish to bring in a consultant who would in-terview prospective and current students to determine why they chose to enroll or not enroll at the institution and why those who enrolled chose to stay or leave. The board approved the project. A trustee made a six-figure gift to fund it. The president involved the faculty in the study. Then, armed with that data, he initiated a pro-cess by which a faculty task force would within six months design a new core curriculum that both honored the college's founding values and spoke to the interests of potential and current students. Some members of the faculty balked at the notion of any curricular change. Others essentially told him that the curriculum was none of his business. A few objected to basing the curriculum on what they considered to be crass marketing. Yet others objected to the time line. But he persisted. In the end, the task force completed its work, and after vigorous discussion, the majority of the faculty approved the change. This president was right. The following year, having effectively marketed the new core to prospective and cur-rent students, the college enrolled a larger freshman class that was of higher quality than in the past. Retention went up. The financial aid discount went down.

When presidents, as is often the case, are confronted with two less-than-desirable alternatives, they need to be creative enough either to come up with a third and better alternative or inspire others to do so. To do the latter, presidents must create for all their colleagues an environment in which they are encouraged to have and advance ideas.

Presidents further serve their institutions and themselves best when they encourage criticism and debate, creating an environment of trust where their colleagues can disagree with them without fear of negative repercussions. Here, I suggest that presidents tell those with whom they work most closely that they, the presidents, count on their colleagues to prevent them from making serious mistakes. I have observed that presidents who do want to brainstorm ideas often find it hard to persuade their colleagues to share their ideas. Too often, their colleagues believe that the president has already decided on a course of action. Therefore, presidents over and over again need to make the point that they are testing ideas rather than pronouncing conclusions. And although this may be hard to achieve, presidents should encourage their closest colleagues to tell them if their presidency is failing. Such candor prevents a president in trouble from being the last to know.

Presidents also need to be careful not to do anything detrimental to their presidency or their institution. As Chapter Five argues, presidents need to recognize that everything they say and do may become a public matter that reflects on the institution. For example, presidents need to be diligent in not confusing themselves with their role, always remembering that they are in demand socially *not* because they are fascinating conversationalists (although they may be that) but rather because of their position. They need to take special care not to confuse the college's resources with their own. Many presidents find themselves traveling in circles of very affluent alumni, trustees, or donors; in these circumstances, they always need to be frugal when spending college money, being cognizant that presidents who spend extravagant amounts on travel or entertaining not only harm the institution they have pledged to serve but do so at their own peril. In his 2010 book *Lead or Leave: A Primer for College Presidents and Board Members*, published by Hamilton Books, two-time college president Roger Hull makes a strong argument that presidents should not spend college funds on items that might be construed as "personal gain." Specifically, he tells presidents, "You need, therefore, to think hard about how badly you want to stay in an expensive hotel or how important a particular renovation to the president's house is. And if it is that important to you, you might at the very least consider spending your own money" (p. 83).

The Institution's Mission

One of a president's most important responsibilities is to allocate precious and often scarce resources, both human and financial. To do so, they usually need to choose among compelling albeit competing claims. Here, the institution's mission should be the touchstone. Specifically, presidents should make mission-driven decisions rather than arbitrary ones, decisions that are also informed by data and considered judgment rather than based on intuition or whim.

The commitment to mission is no small matter. It should drive:

- How resources are allocated

- The campus master plan

- The nature of capital projects

- Personnel decisions (including hiring, tenure, and promotion)

- Institutional policies and practices in such areas as admissions, financial aid, and governance

- Fundraising goals

- Marketing

- Branding

- How the president allocates his or her time

Planning

A clearly understood and well-defined mission also drives the institution's strategic plan, which in turn defines its long- and short-term strategic imperatives and priorities. In the absence of a strategic plan, the annual operating budget by default becomes the institution's chief planning document, a circumstance that invites ad hoc decision making.

Presidents therefore need to require that all plans, strategic and operational, are the product of careful and comprehensive cost-benefit analyses and are based on an understanding of the external environment. Or to put it another way, good plans anticipate as best they can the financial implications, short- and long-term, of the initiatives they contemplate.

Presidents also have the responsibility of articulating the institution's strategic plan and inspiring others to believe that the plan is worthy and feasible. To this end, presidents should regularly inform the trustees and the campus community of the anticipated consequences of decisions contemplated in the plan in such areas as admissions, retention, financial aid policies (particularly the financial aid discount), level of tuition and fees, net tuition revenues, institutional positioning, alumni relations, relationship with the local community, and fundraising. They need to make clear to the trustees and the campus not only the potential benefits of particular decisions but also the associated risks. Finally, they need to educate their boards and campuses about how their institution compares to peer and aspirant institutions.

When a college or university faces financial challenges, there is special urgency in developing a timely and fiscally responsible strategic plan based on realistic assumptions and followed by operational plans that derive from it, such as a three- to five-year financial plan, a fundraising or campaign plan, an enrollment plan, and a marketing plan.

The Board's Role and Responsibilities

To help ensure a president's success, trustees cannot simply assume that once they've selected a president, everything will go smoothly. Rather, every board, and especially its leadership, needs to provide the new president with appropriate support, guidance, and oversight. Here, there is a delicate balance. On the one hand, trustees would be ill advised to involve themselves in operational matters, which are unhesitatingly a presidential responsibility. On the other hand, trustees do not serve their institution if they unreflectively rubber-stamp all presidential recommendations. What board members need to do is to take responsibility and exercise considered and collective judgment.

Both boards and presidents need to recognize that the board is the president's most important constituency because without the support of an informed and dedicated board, no president will succeed. This is a more complicated issue than it might seem because the faculty, the students, the staff, and the alumni all believe to varying degrees that they have primacy. (Every president can tell stories about students who in moments of disagreement assert that they are paying the president's salary.) Parents, members of the local community, and members of both the state and federal government also have claims on presidential time and attention. But courting one or more of these groups at the expense of the relationship with the board or ignoring the board can, as some of the examples in Chapter One illustrated, be fatal.

Most college and university trustees agree to serve on boards for the best motives. Alumni want to give back to their alma mater. Current or former parents have a stake in the success of the institution that has enrolled their sons and daughters. Members of the local community serve because they recognize the importance of the college or university to that community.

Nevertheless, some trustees believe that by showing up for occasional meetings and writing an occasional check they have fulfilled their responsibilities as trustees. They have not been educated about the significance and scope of their responsibilities. They are generally unaware of the complexities of running a college or university today.

The Board and the External Environment

In today's complex higher education environment, boards must first understand the external landscape and see themselves as the president's partner in advancing the institution and fostering an institutional culture of nimbleness. For instance, boards need to understand the implications of the institution's admission policies on such matters as student quality and diversity (ethnic, geographic, gender, and perspective). They need to be educated that high school grades have risen significantly over the last four decades. For example, they need to understand that according to *The American Freshman: National Norms Fall 2010*, written by John Pryor et al. for the Higher Education Research Institute (HERI) at UCLA, 48.4 percent of freshmen who entered college in fall 2010 had graduated high school with straight A averages, only 4.2 percent had C averages, one-tenth of 1 percent had D averages, and the rest had B averages. In contrast, *The American Freshman: National Norms for 2003*, written by Linda J. Sax et al. for HERI, reported that in 1968, only 17.6 percent of college freshmen had straight A averages and 23.1 percent had average grades of C plus or below. In other words, they need to understand that this unbridled grade inflation makes it difficult for admissions offices to give much credence to grade point averages and that grade inflation has also, as the 2010 report from the National Survey of Student Engagement stated, led students to study only fifteen hours per week, less than in previous years and only half as many hours as faculty expect. They need to recognize that this decline in the number of hours students study has had a significant impact on how demanding the curriculum can be and how rigorous course requirements can be, as well as on student learning and behavior. Trustees also need to understand the arguments for and against requiring standardized test scores for admissions and financial aid.

In addition, trustees need to understand that much of what students and parents see as value-added is incredibly costly. The list of expectations usually includes single rooms (at least for juniors and seniors), particular kinds of food served from early morning until well into the night, state-of-the-art fitness centers, and counseling for such problems as excessive drinking, eating disorders, and depression. Students and parents have also come to expect staff to provide academic support, career planning and placement services, opportunities for internships, computer labs that are open around the clock, extended library hours, rich and varied study abroad opportunities, and volunteer programs.

Differences Between Colleges and Other Organizations

It is also essential that trustees understand how colleges and universities differ, in profound ways, from the organizations with which most trustees are associated.

The primary difference is that, unlike in most for-profit organizations, the purpose of colleges and universities is not to produce products or deliver services as efficiently and cost-effectively as possible. Quite the contrary, the better a college, the more faculty and staff members it employs per student, the smaller the class size, the greater the number of students who study abroad, and the greater the number of independent study and research projects that faculty members provide. Similarly, the better a college, the more ample its library, the more sophisticated its technology, the more generous its financial aid, and the more attractive and well maintained its buildings. In fact, even students enrolled at the most prestigious (and often the most expensive) colleges who pay full tuition are not paying the full cost of their education but are being subsidized by college funds and donor gifts.

For-profit organizations often benchmark for efficiency. Colleges measure the opposite, as do the college guides. For example, as Robert J. Morse and Samuel Flanigan explain in their piece, "How We Calculate the Ratings" in the US News & World Report (US News) 2011 Edition of Best Colleges, the rankings favor institutions that have classes of under twenty students, few classes with more than fifty students, average faculty compensation adjusted for regional cost of living differences, low student-to-faculty ratios and the percentage of full-time faculty (pp. 86–87). Institutions with relatively light "teaching loads" are more desirable to faculty than those with greater expectations for in-class time, as are institutions that offer generous support for travel and research, excellent libraries, and state-of-the-art technology.

This very different paradigm is sometimes hard for board members to appreciate. For instance, the board of a prestigious national liberal arts college took pride in the fact that, compared to the college's peers, their staff was very lean. But the staff, faculty, and students had a very different view. The staff was exhausted, trying to meet the needs of the faculty, who felt underserved. The students appreciated the hard work of the staff but were unhappy that the level of staff support was inferior to that at the competitor institutions their friends attended.

It is also not uncommon for some trustees to argue that hiring, tenure, and curricular decisions should be based solely on finances—that is, whether a program generates more revenue than it costs. Their argument usually goes like this: the academy can no longer afford to do things the way that it always has, colleges and universities are endangered species, and liberal arts colleges and programs in particular are facing extinction. To survive, these trustees often argue, colleges should only offer courses that are marketable to students and make sense economically for the college to run. Some further argue for larger classes, heavier teaching loads, more online education, and accelerated degree programs. (In my experience, once these trustees understand that the sciences and the arts cost a great deal more to teach than the humanities, and once they think about the importance of the sciences and the arts both to the larger society and to the college's admissions success, they tend to abandon this approach to the curriculum.)

Board members often have difficulty with the notions of tenure and of shared governance too. Whereas faculty members tend to see tenure as guaranteeing academic freedom, trustees may see tenure instead as an unacceptable mechanism that guarantees lifetime employment for faculty members who do not have to be accountable for their performance (or lack thereof). Whereas the faculty sees shared governance as a way of assuring fairness, integrity, and deliberate informed decision making, trustees often view shared governance as unnecessarily requiring time-consuming, inefficient, and constituency-driven processes. Indeed, at dysfunctional institutions, trustees often view the faculty as unproductive obstructionists. In contrast, in healthy institutions trustees view the faculty with respect and appreciation.

At the same time, members of the campus community need to appreciate that some aspects of colleges and universities should be profitable. They also need to understand that those profits often support the academic programs. For instance, such auxiliary enterprises as residence halls, foodservice, and conference services are profit centers whose revenues support such things as faculty salaries, the library, and instructional technology. Many campus operations also function like businesses. Foodservice runs restaurants and offers catering. Residence halls function like hotels (although without room service). The grounds crew functions as a landscape company, and campus maintenance operates like a construction company, employing electricians, plumbers, carpenters, and locksmiths, for example. Colleges also have their own purchasing offices, public relations operations, and technology support staff.

The Importance of Clear Expectations

In my experience, trustees best contribute to a president's success by immediately arriving at a shared understanding with the president about which decisions belong to the president and which belong to the board. They have come to an agreement about the nature of president-board communications. They also benefit from having similarly candid and in-depth conversations annually about their expectations of one another. Such conversations enable presidents to share with the board their sense of internal and external challenges as well as opportunities. The trustees, in turn, are given the opportunity and responsibility to ask hard questions about those challenges and opportunities and to share with the president their best thinking, so that the board and president can work together to advance the institution.

Key Responsibilities

The most important responsibility of the board of trustees is—with significant input and even leadership from the president—to determine the college's mission. Then, based on the recommendation of the president, who has consulted with the appropriate constituencies, the board approves the college's strategic priorities and its fundraising goals. In so doing, the board creates a context in which the institution can achieve its highest aspirations.

The board also has clear fiduciary responsibilities, including but not limited to:

- Establishing policies that govern the operation and management of the college

- Ensuring that those policies are consistent with current law

- Protecting the college's physical, financial, and other assets

- Overseeing investment of the endowment

- Approving fundraising priorities and goal

- Determining the debt level

- Approving the annual operating and capital budgets, including annual tuition and fees, the financial aid discount, endowment spending, and faculty and staff compensation

Boards need to ensure that the ways the institution allocates resources and defines its fundraising goals are consistent with the mission and designed to achieve the institution's strategic goals. They need to require that the institution's chief planning documents are both strategic and feasible.

The board also has ultimate responsibility, almost always based on the recommendations of the faculty, the chief academic officer, and the president, for granting degrees to those students who meet the college's requirements and overseeing the quality of its academic programs and policies. They usually review and approve the president's recommendations for faculty tenure and promotion. Some boards review and approve college policies on admission and financial aid.

Trustees are also expected to contribute financially, making it one of their top two or three philanthropic priorities, and during a major campaign, their top priority. They should also routinely and generously support the annual fund. In addition, trustees normally should be asked to identify, cultivate, and ideally, solicit potential donors.

Finally, trustees are expected to advise the president, evaluate the president's performance annually, determine appropriate presidential compensation, and review and take action on the president's recommendations for the administrative officers' compensation. The board should support the president both internally and publicly as long as the president has its confidence.

To put it another way, effective trustees intentionally promote presidential success, and presidents see the board as supporters and advisers. To establish this positive relationship, I suggest that, before beginning a presidential search, the board either reaffirm or redefine the institution's mission so that the search committee seeks candidates whose values and whose goals for the institution are consistent with that mission. If a board is looking for a president who will lead the process of changing or refining the institution's mission and goals, then the trustees need to be explicit in charging the search committee with finding candidates who can play that role.

I also recommend that the institutional profile—usually drafted by a search consultant after extensive conversations with all constituencies (such as students, faculty, staff, alumni, and trustees), then vetted and improved by the search committee and approved by the board leadership—provide a guidepost to the president for his or her actions during the first several years and suggest the criteria that the board will use to evaluate presidential performance. For example, if the institution is in the midst of a faltering strategic planning process, the board might ask the president to work with the campus to complete that process during the first year and then recommend to the board a slate of fundraising priorities that would derive from that plan. If the college has suffered from declining enrollments and increasing attrition, the board might make admissions and retention two of the president's top priorities. If town-gown relationships are frayed but important, the board might ask the new president to take an active role in the community and create mutually beneficial partnerships with organizations in the community.

Creating a Board-President Partnership

Once a new president is selected, the board leadership and the president need to begin a partnership.

The Board

To begin, I believe that the following are important:

Experienced People

In consultation with the president, the board should ask several experienced trustees who know and love the institution to serve as advisers to the new president on, for example, how to deal with controversies, difficult personnel matters, and legal issues. Such a group might also advise the president on handling a problem group on campus, gently transitioning out a long-serving vice president who is resistant to change, communicating from day one with the board, and structuring board meetings most effectively, for example.

Presidential Coach

The board should encourage first-time presidents or those whose presidencies are troubled to retain a successful former president as a coach. Effective coaches provide presidents with a safe place to discuss problems and brainstorm solutions.

Review Committee

A formal trustee committee should be designated to evaluate the president's effectiveness annually; the evaluation should include constructive recommendations. At the very least, I suggest that, every summer, the president propose in writing his or her top five to six priorities for the coming year as well as ongoing priorities. In this same document, the president should assess the progress or lack of progress toward meeting the previous year's goals, in the latter case explaining why. After the discussion, the trustees and the president should agree on a final slate of presidential priorities that they then share with the full board at its next meeting.

Outside Consultant Review

At the beginning of a new president's tenure, the board should lay out any plans for a comprehensive 360-degree presidential review to be carried out by an outside consultant. Such reviews are generally conducted no earlier than at the end of the president's third year. For such reviews, the consultant will ask for confidential assessments of the president's performance from those to whom the president reports (that is, the trustee leadership and often the entire board), those who report directly to the president, faculty leaders, administrative program directors, and representative members of the hourly staff and students. Depending on the institution's wishes and culture, consultants may interview a small number of individuals in person, conduct phone interviews, or use online surveys. The consultant will promise that these individuals will not be identified; instead, the consultant will prepare a summary report that identifies none of the participants. Some campuses may wish to expand the list of those being asked for assessments to include members of the community or public officials with whom the president interacts.

Because trustees among themselves may have different expectations about what they wish to know and the decisions for which they want responsibility, the board leadership and president should come to a mutual understanding about at least the following matters:

- What sort of budgetary authority will the board delegate to the president, including types of expenditures, and at what level will the president need trustee approval?

- Which presidential decisions (for example, personnel changes and appointments in the senior administration, approaches to and settlements of litigation or actions that might cause controversy on the campus or with the alumni) need to rise to the level of trustee attention?

- Which matters should be shared with the entire board, the executive committee, a designated board subcommittee, a committee chair, the board chair, or some combination of these?

- If matters of importance occur between board meetings, how should the president communicate them to the trustees and what role should the board chair play in determining that?

- What sort of information does the board wish to receive, how often, and in what form about such matters as admissions, retention, graduation rates, tuition discount, residence hall occupancy, student life, technology, percentage of faculty who are tenured, percentage of students who study abroad, scope of athletics and intramural programs, student involvement in community service, the physical plant, any sustainability initiatives, gifts, the profitability of auxiliary enterprises, and actual expenditures and revenues as compared to budgeted ones?

- What sort of benchmark information based on regional, peer, and next-step institutions does the board wish to receive, and how often and in what form? It is also useful for the board to know the criteria used by the administration in selecting its comparison groups.

- What does the board wish to know about the curriculum? Which curricular changes need board approval? What changes does it want to know about but not act on?

- What does the board wish to know about student life and the co-curriculum? Which changes in these areas need board approval? What changes does it want to know about but not act on?

- What strategic questions will the board regularly ask the president to address?

- Will the trustees expect the administration to explain the information it provides and offer solutions to the problems and challenges it describes?

- Does the board want the president routinely to present the arguments both for and against his or her recommendations, including potential risks and benefits, or does it prefer that she or he advocate for her or his position?

- Will the president and board chair have regular conversations that provide the president—before he or she acts—with input about important matters from the chair, and if the chair so advises, other trustees?

Boards should also seek information about a wide array of other matters. For example, because technology, library materials, utilities, insurance, and—since the 2008 downturn in the market—financial aid costs are rising faster than inflation, presidents need to make the case and boards—as they approve increases in tuition, and room and board year after year—need to understand and be able to communicate to the broader community how these increases will provide value to prospective and current students and their families. The need to make this case is even stronger in today's troubled economy than it was in the past.

The President

Presidents, of course, bear great responsibility for making the relationship with their trustees work. I suggest that, in this relationship, presidents adhere to the following principles.

No Surprises

Presidents must never get ahead of their boards. They need immediately to inform their board chair and trustees about key or controversial issues so that they can decide together what information should be shared with the executive committee and the entire board. No board member wants, for example, to learn about a lawsuit from the local press, about the termination of an employee from that employee, or about a problem in campus life from a parent.

Recommendations

Successful presidents lay the groundwork for recommendations. For example, if a president intends to propose a new science building, she or he needs the board to understand that the project is more than bricks and mortar but rather will dramatically enhance the institution's academic program and competitiveness. Thus, the president might ask members of the science faculty to conduct a board workshop on how teaching science today is different from when they and the trustees were students. At a later meeting, science students—with faculty advisers—might do poster presentations of their research projects for the board, illustrating the effectiveness of student-faculty research projects. Such activities help cultivate trustees who may well decide not only to approve the president's recommendation for the project at hand but also provide personal funding for it.

Strategic Partners

Good presidents see the board as their strategic partner and take advantage of the experience and wisdom of individual trustees.

This is especially true in terms of strategy, establishing priorities, the budget, the physical plant, technology, public relations, legal issues, and personnel matters. Presidents of private colleges and universities and those public institutions not governed by sunshine laws might meet with the trustees alone for an hour at the beginning of each board meeting, sharing with them what keeps them awake at night and asking for their advice on dealing with these problems. The president and the institution will benefit from trustee input, and this conversation will also serve to engage trustees more fully in strategic matters.

Endowment Management

Savvy presidents leave the management of the endowment in the hands of the investment committee. Although presidents should participate in these meetings, this is the one area where the institution and the president both benefit from trustee ownership—even if the president has a degree in economics, business, or finance.

Interaction with Trustees

Successful presidents foster rather than discourage trustee interaction with faculty, staff, and students. In so doing, they demystify the board for the campus and give trustees a personal sense of the qualities and commitment of the faculty, staff, and students. One faculty member at a small, private college had been animated most of his career by his antagonism for and suspicion of the administration and the trustees. After being invited to make a presentation to the trustees and join them for dinner afterward, he recognized that rather than being the indifferent corporate types he had always assumed, they included two of his former students and many other alumni. Although he continued to be critical of presidential and trustee decisions, he no longer attributed to them nefarious motives. Presidents can foster such interaction by doing some of the following:

- Ask members of the campus community to make presentations to the trustees about timely matters followed by a shared meal.

- Ask students and faculty to give presentations to or perform for the board, again followed by a shared meal.

- Create opportunities for trustees to observe classes, rehearsals, athletic events, and student clubs.

- Invite faculty members to host dinners funded by the institution in their homes for small groups of trustees, and perhaps their spouses or partners, along with a few other faculty members. Although trustees might hear complaints, most are sophisticated enough to encourage the person with the complaint to go directly to the president. In addition, if there are problems, it is better that they surface so that the president and his or her colleagues can address them.

Similarly, presidents need to clarify how senior administrators who work directly with trustees should do so, for example, by defining how they wish them to staff trustee committees. For example, if the president wants the board to focus on strategic and policy questions rather than on operational ones, the president and vice president should provide the board with materials that will encourage them to do so. One president complained bitterly that his board was micromanaging renovation projects and was consumed by the minutia of the projects, but it had not occurred to him to direct his financial vice president and the director of facilities to stop making reports to the finance and facilities committee of the board that focused on such minutia. Only when the president began to frame the materials presented to the committee and the board around the larger strategic questions facing the campus—that is, whether it should try to increase the size of the student body, the implications for facilities and quality of doing so, and whether the college should become more residential—did the trustees stop micromanaging.

Clear Roles

As noted earlier, presidents should never confuse their role with that of the trustees. Although trustees admire, respect, and support effective presidents, and although presidents often teach their trustees a lot about higher education in general and the institution in particular, presidents must always remember that they report to the board.

In the end, successful presidents and effective boards recognize the importance of their relationship, and like all partners in a relationship, need to work at it. They need to be intentional about how and what they communicate. They need to be clear about mutual expectations. They need to be candid about problems and concerns. Their ability to establish an effective strategic partnership may well determine whether the institution will thrive.

3

The President and the Campus

Presidents bear great responsibility for establishing positive and productive relationships not only with their board but also with the entire campus. They create community by regularly acknowledging and even celebrating the good work of their colleagues at every level of the institution. For example, they might praise the landscape crew for making the campus especially attractive for parents weekend, homecoming, or commencement at the events themselves and then follow up by personally thanking the staff or by emailing, calling, or sending them handwritten notes. A useful principle: credit goes down and blame goes up, or to put it another way, presidents should credit those lower in the organizational hierarchy for the good things that happen but take responsibility for the negatives.

Presidents should similarly acknowledge the accomplishments of the students and the faculty. And I strongly suggest both avoiding the "royal we" and talking about "my faculty," "my staff," and "my students."

In my experience, the most successful presidents also believe in, articulate, and advance the following notions:

- The academic enterprise is central to the institution's mission.

- Because the education of students includes their lives outside the classroom, students benefit when there is an intentional integration of the curriculum and the co-curriculum.

- Because all members of the faculty and staff contribute to the education of students, they all should first understand the institution's mission and goals and then understand how in their daily work they do in fact help the institution realize its mission and achieve its goals.

- All members of the faculty and staff and student leaders, including residence assistants, should see themselves as retention officers who at the very least know how to advise troubled students about where to go for academic and personal support.

- Senior administrators and the faculty, especially the faculty leadership, should be encouraged to think institutionally and work collaboratively.

- Presidents should always model and—with the exception of personnel and legal matters that require confidentiality—insist on transparency and fulsome communication with the campus and external constituents.

Recommendations for New and Ongoing Presidents

Presidents usually set the tone for their tenure immediately. Thus, within their first year, they either give the campus and the board confidence that they were the right choice or they prompt concerns. What follows are recommendations—some philosophical, some practical—for presidents in their first year and beyond.

The Centrality of Mission

As the previous chapter argues, as a starting point presidents should understand, believe in, and clearly, even eloquently, articulate their institution's mission. They need to ensure that the mission is widely understood, and in an ideal world, embraced by all constituencies, internal and external. Presidents should also explain how the mission is driving the allocation of institutional resources.

Presidents are most likely to achieve campus buy-in if they articulate how the mission is true both to the institution's literal possibilities and its most ambitious but realistic aspirations. Presidents can, and in my judgment, should, provide seed money for initiatives that advance the mission in significant ways. For instance, if a commitment to interdisciplinary studies is part of the institution's mission, the president might fund planning seminars in the summer for faculty who are developing interdisciplinary courses or programs, perhaps by providing participating faculty with stipends, paying for books and supplies, or supporting visiting consultants. If the mission includes global understanding, the president might fund faculty visits to interesting overseas programs to determine whether they should be made available to the college or university's students. If the institution is not currently allowing students to carry institutional financial aid with them for overseas study, the president might ask for a cost-benefit analysis of doing so.

The Importance of Listening

New presidents can immediately signal their desire to understand their campus by announcing that they will meet over their first year with members of various areas of the institution, again to listen and learn. At the same time, by announcing to the campus the timetable and process for the key initiatives they are planning for their first year, presidents communicate the message that they are not merely listening for its own sake but to be able to make informed decisions, and when appropriate, take decisive action. If they intend to begin a strategic planning process, determine the institution's strategic priorities, meet with alumni across the country, or begin planning for a campaign, for example, they should so inform the campus.

New presidents should also stress that they genuinely want to hear feedback from colleagues or others about matters at hand. They need to be clear that they have not yet made a decision and genuinely want input from others. If they want to engage in brainstorming, they need again and again to stress that the ideas they are presenting are not in fact ideas to which they are committed but rather ideas they want to explore.

Holding meetings with various campus groups in a congenial setting and if possible with refreshments further indicates the president's interest in wanting to engage in conversation with those present. If there is the possibility that these meetings may deal with contentious matters, refreshments become even more desirable because people tend to be civil when they are breaking bread together.

Except for matters requiring confidentiality, I advocate that new presidents not act unilaterally but rather engage the faculty, staff, students, trustees, and as appropriate, alumni and members of the local community, in conversations about institutional direction and choices, encouraging each of these groups to think of themselves not primarily as representatives of their own constituency but as guardians of the institution's future. In public institutions and on particular issues, presidents must engage the governor, other elected officials, and the legislature as well.

Early in their tenure and beyond, presidents will also win points and learn a great deal by scheduling whenever possible several hours per week to walk around the campus. They will gain even more goodwill by stopping in faculty and staff offices to ask people about their work or by showing up unexpectedly with coffee and donuts when the early shift of facilities, custodial, or foodservice staff arrive. So that these moments don't evaporate in the press of other business, it makes sense to include these walking-around moments as a formal part of the president's schedule.

I further encourage presidents, beginning the moment their appointment is announced and throughout their tenure, to ask everyone they meet what it is that they, the presidents, need to know to be effective. Because those actually doing the work often have the best insights, it is critical to listen rather than talk in these encounters and then follow up with an email, handwritten note, or phone call thanking those with whom they've had conversations.

As often as possible, presidents should hold meetings outside of their office and expect to be interrupted by sidewalk conversations along the way. People who would feel uncomfortable making an appointment to say something will share what is on their minds quite happily and spontaneously in impromptu conversations. It goes without saying that if presidents want to invite such conversations, they will walk alone; an entourage will discourage people from approaching, and even more negatively, create the notion that they are unapproachable. Meeting in offices other than their own also has a practical value: the president can end the meeting simply by leaving.

As valuable as sidewalk conversations are (and they inevitably will happen not just on campus but pretty much anywhere, from restaurants and movie theaters to athletic events), it is critical that presidents not let these conversations be a substitute for formal proposals or for working through normal channels. Thus, it makes sense for presidents to encourage people who have ideas or requests to email the person on campus with primary responsibility for the area pertinent to the topic at hand, suggesting that they also copy the presidents' assistant. Inevitably, some of these sidewalk conversationalists will not follow up, but asking them to send their ideas in writing precludes the phenomenon of the petitioner saying, "I told the president my great idea and nothing happened."

In addition to their efforts to engage the campus as a whole, presidents will benefit from identifying colleagues and trustees whose judgment they trust to be their sounding board, people with whom they can candidly test ideas and who will read and critique their speeches and important memoranda. Presidents should also make it clear, though, not only that they want those with whom they consult to tell the truth but also that they will seriously listen to and take into account (although not necessarily agree with) what they hear. Of course, presidents must never turn on someone who has been a truth-teller; if they do so, others will decide that telling the truth is a mistake. In inviting others to challenge them, presidents lead by example, making it clear that it is good practice for people who disagree with others to do so as long as those disagreements are civil and constructive.

New presidents might also benefit from asking current colleagues which retired faculty and staff best exemplify the institution's values, invite two or three of those named for a one-on-one breakfast or lunch, and then again ask the retirees what they think the president needs to know to be effective. Such retirees are apt to care deeply about their institution, not to have immediate agendas, and to be pleased to be asked for help.

I do have one cautionary note. As presidents seek to make themselves accessible to a great many people, they need to be wary of those who, in the words of my late husband Kenneth Pierce, were the "first to swim out to meet the boat." In my case, Ken was right. Those who came courting immediately with lots of flattery often became the greatest problems. The moral of the story: presidents need to be unfailingly gracious to everyone, but they also need to be cautious about deciding on whom they can rely until they have a sound understanding of the institution and its people.

Some Practical Recommendations About Listening

I encourage presidents to make it a practice to talk with those who drop into their office even if (or especially if) the president is able to give them only a few minutes. This approach in the end will save time because people will appreciate a few impromptu minutes whereas if they had been required to make an appointment, they would arrive expecting at least thirty minutes of presidential time.

I also recommend that presidents have two email addresses— one published for the campus that goes to the president's assistant, and one restricted to a small group of colleagues and perhaps friends and family that only the president reads. The assistant can forward to the president those emails that require presidential attention but forward most of the others to whomever in the institution is appropriate, sending a note to those writing that she or he has done so. For example, the assistant might write, with a copy to the president, "The president has asked me to thank you for writing and to tell you that we have forwarded your email to the person who is responsible for this area and who will, we know, get back to you." The assistant should ask those to whom they refer a question or a decision to get back to the writer of the email with a copy to the president's public email address within a prescribed time and then double-check to be sure they have done so.

If at all possible, presidents should set aside time each day to read email and then answer each one as soon as they read it (just like in the old days when time management gurus told administrators to handle each piece of paper only once). If presidents don't stay on top of emails, they will find themselves facing an ever-growing avalanche of messages that take on increasing importance to the senders because their earlier messages have gone unacknowledged. If a president needs more information or input before giving an answer or making a decision, it is still good practice to respond immediately with something as simple as "Thanks for writing. Once I know whether or not we are able to move forward on this, I'll get back to you."

When setting up meetings, presidents should always ask, and insist that others ask, what voices other than the usual ones need to be heard—that is, who else should be at the table? It is useful early in every decision-making process for presidents to receive feedback from people who oppose their current thinking. Such conversations will either persuade presidents to the opposing point of view or enable them to address their critics' arguments when announcing a decision.

Visibility

In addition to "managing by walking around," presidents should whenever possible be sure to attend campus events such as student and faculty concerts and art exhibits, plays, athletic events, student presentations of research, faculty lectures, and book signings, and follow them up with a brief email or note congratulating those involved. They might give occasional guest lectures in classes. They may also want to encourage student clubs to invite them and attend the first thirty minutes or so of one of their meetings to learn what the group does and to answer questions. They should sit in the student section at athletic events and eat meals at the student center, and if there is one, the faculty and staff dining room.

I will be candid. I always viewed these occasions as one of the perquisites of my job. If a president sees them as a burden instead, perhaps she or he has chosen the wrong career.

Communicating with the Campus and Other Constituencies

Presidents should routinely try to imagine what it is that they know that others would also like to know, and if at all possible, tell them. To do this, they might send the campus periodic updates, begin each academic year or even each semester with a "state-of-the-college" address, and periodically have meetings with smaller groups of faculty, staff, and students. For example, they might meet with faculty department chairs, the members of the faculty senate if there is one, the student heads of clubs and organizations, and the hourly staff.

At the same time, presidents need to remember the rights of individuals to privacy and the confidentiality required in personnel and many legal matters. They need to be attentive as well to tone in both formal and informal communications, whether written or oral. It is always wise for the president to ask at least some of the vice presidents to review drafts. One new president saved himself a problem by renaming what he originally called "a white paper" as a "report from the president" after the vice presidents told him that his successor had produced a very unpopular white paper a year before.

Another new president who wished to celebrate excellent teaching was told that the institutional culture ran against recognizing individuals. In fact, she was astonished to learn that her predecessor had privately given out several teaching awards every year but chose not to publicize the winners since he believed that those who hadn't won would be jealous. Not wanting to be seen as challenging her predecessor and violating campus norms, she persuaded a donor to fund a new faculty award. At her request, his gift carried the stipulation that the winner would be announced at the fall convocation. At that time, she announced the winner, who earned enthusiastic applause. From that point on, she made these announcements and the university publicized widely the winners of all the teaching awards.

Email is a wonderful communication tool if used judiciously. So are presidential websites that offer information about matters of importance to the campus, copies of the president's publications and speeches, and perhaps photos of campus events. Some presidents today write blogs or create Facebook pages. With each of these tools, presidents need to be careful not to create expectations that they cannot keep. To put it another way, they need to be cautious about instituting communications tools unless they are certain they will be able to meet their audience's expectations for timeliness. And again, they need be attentive not only to content but to tone, so they will not have the luxury of writing something quickly.

Presidents should try to answer questions or make decisions about proposed actions as soon as they can. In particular, if they know they are going to say no to something, they should say it quickly. The longer a petitioner has to wait, the greater the anxiety.

To be blunt, although people will, in the end, accept a positive response, when a long-awaited answer or decision is negative the anxiety may well turn to anger. One president had led a new vice president to believe that at the end of his first year the operating budget would include additional funds for new staff positions, new technology, and new programs. Six months later, facing unexpected budgetary problems, the president had to change her mind. The vice president became very bitter, saying that although he would have taken the same position anyway, he had predicated his planning on those additional resources.

When presidents make mistakes (as they inevitably do), they serve themselves and their institution best by acknowledging that they've done so and perhaps explaining what they've learned from those mistakes. In one such instance, a new president was angered by a decision made by a large academic department. That night, she dictated a letter to the department expressing her rage. She did not intend to send it but rather simply wanted to vent. The following morning, she forgot to tell her assistant to delete that part of the tape and went off to a morning of meetings. When she returned, her assistant proudly told her that, hearing the urgency about this matter in the president's voice, she had typed the memo and hand-delivered it to every member of the department! The president sprinted to the department and went door to door to apologize, explaining that she had never intended to send the memo. Her new colleagues were charmed that she came to them individually and turned into some of her biggest supporters.

The President's Office Staff

Presidents do need to think carefully about how they want to organize their office staff and what roles they want those staff members to play in the institution, with the trustees, and perhaps with other external constituents. Whether to have a "chief of staff" or an "assistant to the president" is for each president to decide, taking into account institutional culture and resources. The same is true of whether the president might wish to include a faculty member in the office staff. Presidents should insist that all members of the office staff see their role as facilitators rather than decision makers. For example, one very savvy presidential administrative assistant organized a lunch each semester for the administrative assistants to those who reported to the president. Her ostensible purpose was to thank them for their good work, but she also created a sense of team and camaraderie that served everyone well. In contrast, some staff members in the president's office need to be disabused of the notion that, by virtue of their role, they themselves have significant power. Acting on that belief almost always backfires. Indeed, staff members with inflated senses of themselves often find themselves marginalized by the vice presidents and deans.

Articulating the Institution's Vision

Good presidents, after consulting with the campus and with board approval, define their vision of how the institution will realize its mission. Presidents do this best when, even while looking to the future, their vision honors the institution's history and is consistent with its culture. Their vision must also address the institution's strengths, weaknesses, opportunities and threats, and resources. Or to put it another way, the president's vision must resonate with the institution, be true to its values, and be clear-minded about its realities. Ultimately, of course, effective presidents inspire the larger campus community to believe that the direction they are advocating is the right one.

Developing a Strategic Plan

Presidents are responsible for developing, assessing, and revising strategic plans. The best plans grow out of a transparent, thoughtful, and inclusive process that is grounded in budgetary realities—that is, good data—and is not constituency-driven. Although presidents may delegate the planning process leadership to someone else, usually a vice president or a faculty leader, ultimately they themselves are responsible. The faculty needs to be integrally involved in the parts of the plan that affect the academic programs.

The President and the Faculty

Effective presidents do not bristle when faculty colleagues say, as more than a few are wont to do, that administrators (especially presidents) come and go, but the faculty stays forever. These presidents understand that the tenure of individual faculty members is likely to exceed, sometimes by a great deal, their presidential service. They recognize that the relationships students have with the faculty, staff, and other students, far more than their interactions with the president, are likely to shape their college experience.

Successful presidents also understand and honor the fact that the faculty has primary responsibility for the curriculum (as long as that curriculum is true to the institution's mission and feasible in terms of resources); for establishing academic standards, including graduation requirements; for approving honorary degree recipients; and for recommending the hiring of faculty, tenure, and promotion.

On some campuses, faculty members also help shape admissions and financial aid, research, faculty development, academic computing, student life, diversity, and budget issues. On most campuses, they make recommendations to the chief academic officer, who in turn recommends to the president, who, if the matter is operational, has final authority. If the matter relates to policy, the president seeks board approval.

For their part, most faculty members value presidents who understand and practice shared governance, and are transparent and respect their role and responsibilities. Increasingly, they also value presidents who raise money, understand budgets, and can allocate and reallocate resources and improve the institution's reputation.

But there are times when a president's judgment may run counter to that of the faculty. For example, overturning a positive tenure recommendation is probably the most difficult and contentious decision a president can make. Because on many campuses faculty members at the department level have difficulty saying no to their immediate colleagues, who often are their friends, it frequently falls to presidents—who know that granting tenure essentially guarantees lifetime employment and that granting tenure to an individual who is not genuinely excellent deprives the college of the opportunity to find someone who is—to make the difficult decisions. Because the reason for such a decision must be confidential, presidents are in the difficult position of not being able to explain.

Presidents also have ultimate authority for hiring both faculty and staff. In some institutions, usually smaller ones, they exercise this authority. In larger institutions, they are more apt to delegate that authority to their chief academic officer or to academic deans. Presidents usually can and should trust the judgment of their faculty colleagues and the chief academic officer or dean about the legitimacy and appropriateness of the candidates' credentials. The president is responsible for ensuring either through direct action or through delegation to the chief academic officer that those who are hired understand and appreciate the institution's mission and its values.

Presidents most likely to weather the storms occasioned by difficult personnel decisions are those who have demonstrated genuine interest in and respect for the faculty from the day they applied for the job. As I've already mentioned, they show interest in the work of the faculty and students by attending, as possible, lectures, concerts, performances, and art exhibits. They know faculty members informally, perhaps by hosting occasional breakfasts, lunches, and dinners for small groups, always with the goal of listening and learning. They engage the faculty on matters of institutional importance, genuinely seeking their counsel. If they have a disagreement with a faculty member, they do not become defensive but try to understand (perhaps again through informal conversation) the basis for that disagreement. Whether they ultimately agree or not, most faculty members will appreciate a president's genuine efforts to find common ground.

Of course, such efforts do not always work. For example, an assistant professor for whom I'd taught several classes as a guest lecturer refused to sit next to me at the annual faculty dinner even though she was ahead of me in the buffet line. Her explanation: several of her colleagues would accuse her of being an "apple polisher" if she did. I assured her that it was fine for her to sit elsewhere and then reminded her gently that I was a colleague too.

There are also some members of the faculty who on principle will not work constructively with the president or others in the administration. One of my colleagues opposed every administrative decision in which he was not personally involved, even if the appropriate faculty committees had recommended or approved it. Believing that he was the center of, if not the universe at least the university, he often insisted that if he had not been consulted, no one had been consulted. When confronted with such obstructive behavior, presidents do well to remember that one of the things that faculty members are valued for is their independent thinking. As one of my colleagues put it, "Faculty choose to become academics because they think otherwise."

Giving the Faculty the Right Information

In addition to whatever state-of-the-college address presidents give to the campus community, I encourage every president to begin the academic year and perhaps every semester with an extended conversation (perhaps four hours, perhaps an entire day) with the faculty about matters of institutional importance. When inviting them, the president should make it clear that the conversation will not be a formal faculty meeting governed by *Robert's Rules of Order* nor a forum for regular faculty business. Instead, this conversation will be designed to provide an opportunity for informal brainstorming and give-and-take between the faculty and the administration. Holding the conversation in a different venue than that used for formal faculty meetings, as well as serving food at breaks and perhaps box lunches for breakout group conversations, will further differentiate this conversation from regular faculty meetings.

Such conversations might be organized around topics such as a new strategic planning or master planning process, the pressures on the budget, the relationship between the curriculum and the cocurriculum, the goals of a future capital campaign, enrollment and retention, or the most desirable size for the institution. The conversations serve a twofold purpose. First, they inform the faculty about the state of the institution and explain the context, both internal and external, for administrative and board decisions. Second, the president and members of the administration benefit from hearing the faculty's thoughts about decisions that are yet to be made. In other words, what is most important in these conversations is that the president and vice presidents both be forthcoming with pertinent information and actually listen to and take into account what faculty members are saying. In some instances, the president might bring in an outside expert to provide a broader context for the discussion. In other cases, the president or vice presidents may provide that context, as long as they keep their presentations brief.

Shared Governance

Because every campus culture is, as I've noted earlier, idiosyncratic, so is the way that the institution practices shared governance. But some notions are pretty standard, particularly those that derive from the *Statement on Government of Colleges and Universities*, 1966, which was later adopted by the American Association of University Professors, the American Council on Education, and the Association of Governing Boards (section 4, paragraph 4).

For example, it is standard practice for the board to charge the president with developing a vision for the future, a slate of evolving strategic priorities, and fundraising plans. It is also standard practice for the board to delegate functions and powers it considers appropriate to the president and through the president to subordinate administrative officers and the faculty. The president is also usually charged with ensuring that the institution adheres operationally to standards of sound academic practice and ensures that, in the areas of shared governance, the board understands the full range of faculty views and the faculty understands the decisions and views of the board.

Moreover, just as the board delegates responsibility for leading and managing the institution to the president, the board and the president delegate primary responsibility for the curriculum, methods of instruction, degree requirements, research, faculty status, and those aspects of student life that relate to the educational process, to the faculty. According to the AAUP document, here the president and the board normally "concur with the faculty judgment except in rare instances and for compelling reasons." In such instances, it is good practice for the president to explain to the faculty the reason for such a decision.

What does vary from campus to campus is how these notions are implemented. On some campuses, the president chairs the faculty meetings; on others, the provost, the academic vice president, the academic dean, or a faculty member takes the role of chair. Some institutions have faculty senates. On some of those campuses, it is customary for the president to interact with the faculty senate; on others, the faculty senate operates separately from the president, often working with the chief academic officer. Some faculties meet as a whole monthly, others less often. Some may meet more often. On some campuses, the president, the chief financial officer, and the chief academic officer shape the annual operating budget. On some campuses that group includes all the vice presidents. On yet others, faculty, staff, and students are members of the group crafting the budget, which it then recommends to the president, who in turn recommends it to the board. Faculty participation in board meetings varies from campus to campus too. On some campuses, they have no role at all; on others, they serve on trustee committees and have at least one representative serving ex officio on the board, often with voice but not vote.

My own favorite story about faculty governance comes from a president who no longer wanted to chair faculty meetings so that she could participate in the discussions more easily. She brought this up with the faculty, making it clear that she would be content for either the provost or the chair of the faculty senate to chair the meetings. The faculty deliberated for several months and then voted down her request, with faculty leaders telling her privately that many of them feared that if she no longer chaired faculty meetings, she would stop attending them.

But no matter how campuses practice shared governance, what is important is that the president not only communicate regularly with the faculty but also actively engage and listen to those faculty selected by their peers to be in leadership positions during conversations about matters of academic importance.

The President and the Staff

I recommend that presidents hold a variation on the faculty conversation with staff members. The goal here is similar: to share information with the staff about matters of institutional importance and listen to their ideas. To accommodate staff members who work different shifts, presidents might offer two sessions of perhaps ninety minutes each. Again, I encourage the president to describe briefly the state of the college and then listen to the thoughts about impending decisions. Because some staff members hesitate to ask questions publicly, in advance of these meetings the president might invite the staff to email questions or even send them anonymously by campus mail.

Staff members often feel second-class to the faculty, but good presidents recognize their value to the institution, students, faculty, alumni, and more. Indeed, staff members on the proverbial front lines are often the ones who work most closely with students. Some of the best "retention officers" I have known were hourly employees who came to know students in the course of their daily work. For example, an especially outgoing custodian persuaded many students not to drop out of school, telling them how privileged they were to be in college and that they needed to graduate if they didn't want to end up, as he put it, "behind a broom." To his great pride, this man's two daughters both graduated from the college that employed him. Another custodian in a residence hall wrote op-ed pieces for the student newspaper, encouraging the students whom she called "her kids" to work hard and graduate. On one occasion, the students thanked her by cooking a spaghetti dinner for her and the president in their dorm room—on a hot plate, no less. A groundsperson was even more explicit about his role, explaining that his job was more than keeping the campus looking beautiful—it was also admissions and retention.

Staff members often bring forward the best ideas. A staff member in the finance area, for example, recommended to her supervisor and then to the president that the university combine the offices of student accounts and financial aid in order to better serve students who, at the time, were being shuttled from one office to the other and back. She explained that, because the times of pressure for each area were different, if they cross-trained the staffs in both functions they would have more people available at these pressured times of year to make awards and assist students and parents. When she became director of the combined areas, she and her colleagues provided better service and became more efficient. Through normal attrition, the new department eventually downsized the staff by five positions.

The President and the Senior Staff

To be effective, presidents need to have colleagues in senior positions who do in fact think institutionally, not functionally, and who think and act strategically rather than just tactically. In other words, these vice presidents and deans need to approach all problems as if they were the president, charged with the well-being of the entire institution and not just the areas for which they are formally responsible.

I believe that presidents are responsible for the way in which the members of the senior staff interact. Those who foster a collaborative rather than a competitive environment encourage their colleagues in the free exchange of ideas. They do not practice a spoke-and-hub approach where the presidents are the hub and each senior administrator works one-on-one with them. They discourage those who report to them from engaging in what may be seen as a kind of sibling rivalry. Rather than ignoring or even encouraging their colleagues to jockey for position or criticize each other, they insist that those who report to them work together to resolve their differences, intervening only when their colleagues are genuinely unable to resolve things to their mutual satisfaction.

Presidents need to be intentional about how they work with those who report to them in other ways too. For example, presidents should not allow their direct reports to "delegate up." Rather, their colleagues should come to them not with problems they want the president to solve and matters they want the president to handle but with recommended solutions to problems and a plan for handling the matter on their own. At the same time, presidents should not act as their own vice presidents. In other words, they need to delegate to those who are responsible for certain areas. To put this another way, presidents need to give their senior staff members not only responsibility but also authority. They also need to be clear about how they wish to work with each of their vice presidents.

Presidents should also give those with whom they work closely the information they need to make their own choices. This is particularly true when it comes to performance evaluations. Just as the trustees need to be clear about their expectations, so presidents need to clearly lay out their expectations for those who report to them. Specifically, I suggest that the president have a conversation with each "direct report" individually and then follow up with a memo, casting their conversation positively but also making their expectations clear. Their memo might go something like this: "I'm glad that we talked this morning about how important it will be for you in the future to do x, y, and z."

If presidents wish to have more direct contact with midlevel administrators without usurping the vice presidents' authority, they might create an advisory group of those who report directly to them and their direct reports. These groups might meet monthly for an hour or two, again with refreshments. The meetings serve two functions: first, as occasions when the president asks for advice and answers questions, and second, as a way to break down silos, because when people get to know each other they are more apt to collaborate. Although this president-staff meeting may seem more congenial to a small campus than to a large one, the dangers for presidential isolation are greatest on a large campus. Therefore, presidents on large campuses should take steps to ensure a mechanism for them to hear directly from people in key positions in an atmosphere where ideas may be exchanged freely. Such meetings can model for these midlevel administrators the kind of collaboration the president values.

When those who work with presidents make a mistake, they should be reassured that, unless the mistake is illegal or unethical or the result of a serious failure of judgment, making a mistake is human. But it is critical that they learn from the experience and not make the same mistake again. For example, one of my colleagues, thinking that she was writing only to me, made a caustic comment about a colleague and then hit "reply all" by mistake. She was mortified and immediately called the other recipient of the email to apologize. She also was worried about my reaction. I encouraged her to see the humor in the situation and assured her that I had previously done the same thing. We agreed that both of us needed to be mindful of email recipients before hitting "send."

The President and the Students

One of the great joys of being on a college campus is the opportunity to be with and get to know students. Although some presidents teach, the increasingly external demands on their time discourage many from doing so. Some presidents conclude that they can find the time to prepare for and actually teach a class, particularly if it meets only once a week. Others determine that it would be almost impossible for them to be available to students outside of class time in desired ways: for individual conversations, extended office hours, and in-depth assessment of papers and exams.

There are many ways other than or in addition to teaching for presidents to interact directly with and get to know their students.

Monthly Meetings

Schedule a monthly meeting with the editor of the student newspaper and any writers that individual wishes to bring along, giving these students the president's private email address so that the students can reach him or her directly if they have questions or want a quote. The time is well spent because it can prevent the publication of misinformation (which inevitably will take time to manage) and give the students the opportunity to share their perspective. Such meetings also give the president the chance to suggest topics for future articles.

Also meet at the beginning of each semester with the members of student government and student media, together with the members of the president's cabinet. The students might be asked to describe their goals for the year and the vice presidents might each outline their responsibilities so that the students know where to go directly for help and don't have to come to the president first.

Monthly Dinners

Host a monthly dinner for thirty or forty students along with at least some of the vice presidents or deans at the president's house or another congenial location. After dinner, ask students an open-ended question like, "What do I need to know?" Presidents and their colleagues can also answer student questions. Such dinners also serve as rumor control. One personal example: when I first arrived at Puget Sound, a student criticized me for turning down what was widely believed to be an offer of support for a new football stadium from a major corporation that manufactured its products overseas. I explained that no such gift had been offered, and there-fore, I had not turned it down. Eleven years later, another student congratulated me for turning down that same gift, praising me for, in his words, "rejecting money earned by exploiting overseas labor-ers." I again explained that no such gift had been offered and that I therefore had not turned it down, but I nevertheless appreciated the praise.

Other Recommendations

Host an occasional program on the student radio station. Work out in the fitness center at times when students are there. Some presi-dents have done even more to get to know students. Some invite students to run with them. Others go into the locker room after athletic events. Some presidents travel with athletic teams when they are on the road.

Managing Risks and Crises

The college president must often deal with unwanted events—from crises such as shootings on campus and natural disasters to events that are serious but affect only a small group of people, such as student parties that disrupt the neighborhood or sexual harassment that causes pain to the victims. There may be illegal actions by a member of the campus community that bring negative publicity to the institution, bomb threats, or terrible individual tragedies that affect a great many people on campus, such as a student death.

So it's good practice for presidents to work with their staff colleagues, key members of the human resources staff, the trustees, and legal counsel to develop a comprehensive risk management plan including a process for making rapid but considered decisions. All involved need to understand that the plan might and probably will need to be modified in real circumstances. For instances when there might be adverse publicity, the institution's public relations officer should prepare a communications plan. If the publicity surrounding an event is likely to be especially damaging to the institution, the president should consider bringing in an outside public relations firm skilled in damage control.

Terrible shootings on college campuses and major natural disasters, like Hurricane Katrina, especially require deliberate, decisive, and immediate action to ensure the safety of those on campus. In these kinds of instances, it is essential that the president not only take a leadership role but also be perceived to be doing so. Such events also require the president to lead efforts to help the campus heal. Here, presidents should involve the campus community, including students and faculty members, in planning and implementing follow-up activities.

Risk management plans should include answers at least to the following questions:

- If the president is away from campus, who will be the decision maker?

- Where will people meet if the campus itself hasn't been damaged? Where will they meet if it has been damaged?

- How will the administration communicate with those on campus? With commuting students, faculty, staff, trustees, and alumni who may not be on campus at the time of the crisis? With parents? And if appropriate, with local law enforcement and public officials?

- What contingencies are in place if the phone lines and the internet are knocked out? For example, has the campus entered into an arrangement with a campus in a distant location to host its website if necessary?

Crises and Public Relations

The most difficult crises are, of course, those that would damage the institution if they became public. In my experience, the best policy is for the campus to be as forthcoming as it can be with information that is not confidential. For example, one president was confronted with a potential public relations disaster when a student's parents threatened to sue the college, accusing a security officer of using unnecessary force when restraining their son, who had physically threatened his roommate. The president hired a highly respected former prosecutor to investigate, and on the advice of the college's attorney but against the advice of several vice presidents, promised the parents that she would share the investigator's report with them. The college also developed additional training for the staff and described the training to the parents. The investigator's report found that the security officer had in fact acted inappropriately. In the end, the parents decided not to sue because they were impressed with the president's candor, the report, and the new training. Perhaps even more importantly, they learned details about their son's behavior that they did not want made public.

The internet and social media make the threat of negative publicity especially potent. In one highly publicized case, a white student posted a video on YouTube denouncing a group of minority students. The video went viral, as did a second video denouncing the maker of the first video. Because of the potential impact of such moments on admissions and fundraising, some campuses have staff that do nothing but monitor the internet for references to their institution in order to counter such negative messages.

Unfavorable Personnel Decisions

Because decisions to terminate an employee, deny tenure or promotion to a faculty member, or terminate a program that would in turn result in layoffs all carry the risk of litigation and negative publicity, presidents would be wise to require that advance notice of all proposed terminations, the reasons for them, and the process to be followed, be shared either with them or someone to whom they have delegated this responsibility. This gives the institution time to consult with legal counsel to be sure that the decision is fair and that institutional policies, applicable laws, and appropriate processes are being followed. It also gives the institution time to prepare a press release or have answers for the press if the action becomes public. At the same time, institutions are often hampered in dealing with such crises precisely because they need to protect the confidentiality of one or more of the people involved.

In those (one hopes rare) circumstances that might become volatile, it is good practice to inform campus security and have security officers in the area. I know of one instance when the presence of security officers prevented a terrible tragedy because they were able to stop an employee who had just been terminated from shooting his supervisor.

Although litigation over decisions not to hire someone is rare, if the hiring officer believes that litigation or negative publicity might result, the officer should follow this same advice.

The President and the Local Community

In the last several decades, many colleges and universities have focused on creating partnerships with the local community. In some cases, the institution seeks to develop the relationship to address negative perceptions of their neighborhood. Other college-community partnerships are inspired by the institution's desire to foster civic engagement among their students by having them volunteer in the community and by the growing national interest in service learning, which ties experiential learning with the classroom. Yet other colleges and universities find themselves at odds with the cities in which they are located because of destructive student behavior. And yet others seek such partnerships because they wish to expand and need the support of their community to do so.

What characterizes many of these efforts is the willingness of the colleges and universities to invest their own funds in the community and take a comprehensive approach, focusing on urban development, the schools, crime, and housing. They often create partnerships with corporations and city government to fund particular projects.

As impressive as many of these efforts have been, as Frances Lawrence notes in his introduction to essays by former presidents in *Leadership in Higher Education: Views from the Presidency* published in 2006 by Transaction Publishers, other efforts have been troubled and led to the termination of the president who inspired them. Thus, even though the rewards of such partnerships are many, when the partnerships require significant financial commitments, presidents and boards should heed Lawrence's warning that "the line between success and failure in the public, politically sensitive arena of urban development is obviously a tightrope not easily negotiated and the penalties for a mistake are painful for presidents and institutions alike" (p. 2).

Before embarking on a partnership with the community that requires significant institutional funds, presidents and boards should do a cost-benefit analysis that asks the following questions:

1. Will the partnership advance the institution's mission?
2. Will it contribute to educational opportunities for students; research opportunities for faculty or students; career preparation for students; admissions and retention; improved town-gown

relationships; the institution's reputation; new revenue for the institution, among other things?

3. What are potential liabilities for the institution of the proposed partnership?

4. What will be the start-up and the ongoing costs, both financial and human, and can the institution afford these costs?

The President's Time

Because the president's time is one of every institution's most precious commodities, it needs to be allocated with intentionality and care. Those who report to the president have a special responsibility to use the president's time well.

The senior staff, for their part, should ask for the president's time only when the occasion demands it—that is, only when no one other than the president can assume responsibility. They also need to prepare the president as fully as possible for each event and action, as they do so thinking as if they were the president. For example, I would advise staff members not to do what one of my colleagues did during the first months of my presidency: arrange an alumni event in a singles bar where the only way I could be seen and heard was to stand on a table! Nor would I advise them, as happened to one new president, to send the president across the country to thank an alumnus for a major scholarship. At the dinner, the president learned that the alumnus had not funded the scholarship and had no intention of doing so.

Members of the alumni relations and development and admissions staff who work with the president's office should coordinate their events to maximize the president's time when he or she is in a particular location in order to cut down on unnecessary travel. For example, at the beginning of each summer, the president's assistant might create a calendar for the year that notes those days when the president must be on campus: during homecoming, commencement, and board meetings, for example. The president, the assistant, perhaps other members of the president's staff and the key people in alumni relations, development, and admissions might then meet to decide which days each month, preferably clustered together, the president could dedicate to external matters. It is then up to the staff to propose a schedule to the president. The group might repeat the same exercise in January with an eye to revising the travel schedule if it makes sense to do so.

Members of the senior staff should also, at least a day or more before individual or small group meetings with the president, provide the president with an agenda and pertinent materials. This allows the president time to think about the matters and be able to answer questions or make decisions during the meetings themselves rather than having to meet again to do so.

It goes without saying that vice presidents and deans should always remember that presidents have myriad demands on their time. Therefore, these senior staff members need to be immediately responsive to presidential requests and require members of their own staffs to do the same.

Presidents also should remember that people usually become administrators because they want to make their colleges and universities better places. Thus, they care a great deal and take problems very much to heart. Here, my advice is simple: presidents should remember and remind those who report to them that today's crisis will inevitably be replaced by tomorrow's crisis. If they are anxious, they shouldn't show it, because their demeanor will influence the behavior of those around them. If they are calm and thoughtful, others are more likely to be calm and thoughtful too.

As this chapter suggests, it can be daunting to work with multiple constituencies. To do so effectively, presidents need to surround themselves with excellent colleagues to whom they can delegate. This group includes the senior administrators who report to the president, staff members in areas such as development, alumni relations, admissions, and public relations who have a claim on presidential time, members of the president's office staff, and if there is a president's house, the staff there. If these colleagues are to succeed, presidents need to be explicit about their expectations for each of them. They need to describe clearly how they wish to work with them. They need to give them genuine authority as well as responsibility. And when their colleagues fulfill their roles well, they need to acknowledge that. But perhaps most importantly, presidents need to set priorities and be disciplined in how they use their own time as well as the time of others.

When presidents become leaders of an effectively functioning team, they can enjoy the pleasures of being a president, and even have fun—something that will be the subject of the final chapter.

4

Nothing Happens Until Money Happens

A lmost every presidential search committee with which I have worked in the last several years has begun by talking about money. They all want their next president to be both an effective manager of the institution's financial resources and a superb fundraiser. In their quest for someone who can allocate or reallocate funds wisely and fairly, and can raise a good deal of money, some committee members have gone so far as to argue that they would be content with a president who fulfilled these two responsibilities and were compelling as the public face of the institution. They based this argument on their belief that people other than the president can and even should run the institution. For example, I've heard committee members argue that the chief academic officer can take care of the faculty and the academic programs, the student affairs officer can handle everything that has to do with students, the enrollment management officer can be in charge of admissions and retention, and so on.

When committees assume that the institution would benefit from a president who devotes her- or himself primarily to the budget, fundraising, and public speaking, I usually explain that in my experience the most successful presidents are those who do all of this and more. I describe presidents who are able to make sound budgetary decisions and raise a great deal of money precisely because they truly understand the academic and co-curricular programs.

They are also able to tell the institution's story persuasively and articulate its aspirations and needs in ways that make that story and those needs and aspirations come alive to donors and external constituents.

Many trustees also want a president who is entrepreneurial and can think outside the proverbial box. Some hope the individual will generate new revenue-producing ventures, such as online, off-site, and adult education programs. Some desire partnerships with other colleges and universities, local businesses, and the local community that will lead to operational efficiencies, income-producing programs, or simply goodwill.

The President and the Budget

Wise boards want their president to ensure that financial and human resources are dedicated to supporting the institution's mission and advancing its priorities. Thus, although such boards do and should provide extensive fiduciary oversight, they usually delegate the primary responsibility for the institutional budget to the president. That having been said, most boards expect the president to share with them benchmarking that places their institution's revenues and expenses in the context of peer and aspirant institutions. They generally want to see rolling three- to five-year financial plans that conservatively project both revenues and expenses. They want to be sure that the institution is complying with all applicable regulations and laws. They also generally assume that such auxiliary operations as foodservice, residence halls, and conference services will produce surpluses that will support the academic programs.

At the outset of budget planning, presidents need to be sure that the projected revenues and expenses are realistic. In some instances, such as some benefits and debt service, these numbers are absolute. The projected amount of income from the endowment is usually based on a board-approved formula. Such budgetary assumptions as numbers of students enrolled and percentage of students living on campus are likely to derive from past data. In other cases, the vice presidents—based on their own careful analyses and in collaboration—need to advise the president on the implications of various levels of tuition, room, board, fees, and financial aid not just for the budget but also for admissions, retention, and campus life generally. Similarly, the appropriate vice presidents need to explain the implications of various salary levels and benefits not just for the budget but also in terms of how they compare with peer institutions. The vice president for advancement needs to project the amount of money that the annual fund will contribute to the operating budget. The entire group needs to work together to project dollar amounts for capital projects, maintenance, depreciation, debt service, technology, and the library.

Armed with this information, the president can then give guidance to those who craft the budget and those with a formal role in making budget requests, clearly explaining the level of expenses the president can accept based on the anticipated revenues. She or he also needs to identify the amount of contingency fund to be included in the operating budget. The president also needs to give colleagues guidance in those areas where decisions must be made, such as tuition, fees, and financial aid and what numbers she or he is willing to accept and then recommend to the board.

The Budget and Institutional Values

My former colleague Thomas F. Staley, provost at the University of Tulsa in the mid-1980s when I was the dean of Tulsa's College of Arts and Sciences, often said, "While the soul of an institution can be found in its curriculum, its conscience can be found in its budget." Tom's formulation became my mantra. I soon also came to understand that without a strategic plan, decisions will inevitably be made in an ad hoc way, without reference necessarily to mission or strategic priorities. As a result, the operating budget—in addition to reflecting the institution's values—by default determines how the institution will function.

Clarity about mission allows presidents to differentiate between critical and merely desirable initiatives. Puget Sound is a good case study of how this can work. To achieve our goal of becoming a national residential liberal arts college of academic excellence, we committed to enhancing the quality of the student body; improving the student-faculty ratio; creating new facilities and spaces across the campus that would foster conversation between and among student, faculty, and staff; becoming more residential; and enriching the quality of the academic experience and student life. My colleagues and I, and as appropriate the board, gauged every request for new funding against those goals. To enhance the quality of the student body, we also intentionally reduced the budgeted size of the freshman class from 700 to 650 and reduced the number of transfer students, resulting in an increase over time in SAT scores from 1067 to 1253. (Approximately 90 points of this increase were the result of the College Board's 1995 recentering of SAT scores in order to make 500 the average score for the students then taking the exam.) In addition, to improve the student-faculty ratio, we added thirteen new tenure-line faculty positions. We spent $85 million on new construction and major renovations that brought us a new humanities building, a concert hall, a two-hundred-bed suite-style residence hall, a fitness center, a café, and playing fields, as well as a stunning renovated library and a re-created theater. We significantly renovated all our existing residence halls, the student center, and several major academic buildings. Meanwhile, thanks to a successful comprehensive campaign and the ongoing careful use of institutional resources, the endowment grew from $68 million to $213 million. We did not provide support for a host of excellent ideas because, as desirable as they were, they were not central to our primary goals.

The Long-Range Financial Plan

It usually falls to the financial vice president, in consultation with the president and the other vice presidents, to develop a long-range financial plan that is updated annually to reflect any new budgetary realities, such as changes in benefits or utilities. Such plans include the same projected revenues and expenses that populate the annual operating budget. For a long-range financial plan to be useful, it—like the annual operating budget—needs to be based on realistic and conservative assumptions rather than, as happens at some institutions, hopes and dreams. Financial plans should also provide for significant contingencies.

To Borrow or Not to Borrow

In the last several decades, many colleges and universities have engaged in an amenities war. Because their presidents and boards believed the market would continue to rise and were confident that the return on investing those funds would more than cover new debt service, many borrowed heavily to build attractive residence halls, state-of-the-art recreational facilities, and appealing academic buildings. Others borrowed in order to preserve institutional funds, which they assumed would yield more than they needed to pay in the interest on the loans. But such loans often came with substantial new debt service, and there were new expenses associated with operating and maintaining the new facilities. Significant borrowing in some cases also limited future debt capacity.

Roger Hull in *Leave or Lead* argues adamantly that colleges should "pay as you go." He further explains, "I never took on a project without knowing how I could pay for it, and paying for it generally meant going out and raising money" (2010, p. 19). Although institutions might reasonably disagree with Hull's principle, the decision to borrow does need to be made with great care, with the president, and ultimately the board, finding the right balance between current desires and long-term goals.

Compliance

Just as in the private sector, compliance has become an important issue on college campuses. For example, the federal government now requires that both the president and the board take full responsibility for reviewing the 990 form, having a genuine understanding of the financial statements, and keeping up with the latest regulatory pronouncements. Although presidents are not expected to be compliance experts in their own right, they must make it clear to their staff and particularly the chief financial officer that the latter not only must have the necessary expertise but also be absolutely certain that the college is maintaining the required compliance. In fact, this is one of those areas where presidents should call upon trustees who have such expertise to provide oversight.

The Operating Budget

There is no standard process in higher education by which the annual operating budget is built other than that, ultimately, presidents submit the budget to the board for approval. In some cases, the financial vice president crafts the budget and recommends it to the president. In some cases, the financial vice president works closely with the other senior officers in shaping the budget. In some cases, the president leads the process. Some institutions have more collaborative processes involving members of the faculty, staff, and student body. Given the increasing pressures on the budget, I recommend the latter approach because it engenders both trust and greater understanding on the part of the campus community. Indeed, I know of several presidents who fruitfully involved the entire campus in discussions of how their institutions, facing tuition and fundraising shortfalls, should proceed. Although the results were painful each time—in that to balance their budgets the institutions eliminated both positions and programs—the campuses deeply appreciated their president's transparency. They did not like the outcome but they understood why it was necessary.

Financial Aid: A Key Driver of the Budget

Second only to compensation, financial aid is the biggest expense in annual operating budgets. Families are increasingly concerned about costs. The 2010 CIRP freshman survey, sponsored by the Cooperative Institutional Research Program at the Higher Education Research Institute and reported in the 2010 American Freshman National Norms study, revealed that almost two-thirds of incoming students stated that the "current economic situation significantly affected my college choice," with 20 percent saying they "agree strongly" and 42.1 percent saying they "agree somewhat" (p. 8). The study further revealed that 53.2 percent of students with financial need stated that "not being offered financial assistance was a 'very important' factor in choosing which college to attend" compared to only 33.2 percent who reported not being affected (p. 8). Moreover, the financial aid package for 53.1 percent of incoming students included loans, and 73.4 of respondents reported receiving grants and scholarships, the largest percent in the decade since HERI has been asking these questions.

This sensitivity to cost and the competition among colleges and universities to enroll students have put financial aid offices under pressure to offer enough financial aid to attract the best possible students. However, even as many financial aid officers have become sophisticated about constructing an effective financial aid package, they often are not knowledgeable about the institution's larger financial issues. Thus, it is essential that presidents make sure that the financial aid director, the controller, the vice president for enrollment, and the financial vice president work very closely together to predict what the institution will need for financial aid, and even more importantly, recommend to the president what they have agreed, given the institution's resources, will be the actual cost of financial aid (and thus the financial aid discount) for the coming year and the subsequent three to four years.

A Model for Collaborative Budgeting

Variations of the following model have worked well at a number of institutions, including Puget Sound. Campuses almost certainly will want to modify this process based on their institutional culture, but this approach provides a good starting point.

A budget committee, co-chaired by the academic and financial vice presidents with members from the faculty, staff, and student body, are charged with developing a balanced operating budget for the coming fiscal year, which it recommends to the president. Committee members commit to thinking institutionally rather than seeing themselves as representatives of their own constituencies. They also sign a pledge committing themselves to confidentiality during and after the process.

The committee begins its work in the fall with a meeting with the president who outlines any "givens"—that is, additions or subtractions on the expense side that the president wants to be in the recommended budget. These might, for instance, include additional development staff to prepare for a capital campaign or new faculty lines to staff a new core curriculum.

The committee then holds budget hearings, probably weekly, listening to presentations from each of the vice presidents as well as faculty, staff, and student body representatives. The requests are likely to be for new positions, new programs, increased allocations to various lines in departmental operating budgets, and new technology. Students might ask for an increase in student fees. The faculty and staff might focus on salary and benefits. Requests almost certainly will exceed available resources, so the committee will have to establish mission-related priorities.

At the end of the semester, the committee submits its recommended budget to the president, shares it with the entire campus, and then holds separate meetings with interested members of the faculty, staff, and student body to explain recommendations and answer questions. Following those meetings, members of the campus community have two weeks to write the president with their responses, which the president takes into account before bringing his or her own recommendation to the board.

The virtues of this process are several:

- Although inevitably a number of people will be disappointed that their requests are not funded, the transparency of the process and the diverse membership of the committee gives the process credibility. The campus understands that decisions were not made arbitrarily.

- Members of the faculty and staff who serve on the committee gain a deep understanding of how budgeting is done and the pressures on the budget. They are, therefore, able to explain the process and the pressures to their colleagues.

- Presidents have the benefit of understanding the campus sentiment before making their recommendations to the board, allowing them to frame their message in ways that address campus concerns.

The Fundraising President

To be effective fundraisers, presidents need to understand and be able to explain to donors at least the critical importance of the areas most likely to attract external funding:

- Financial aid

- Endowed faculty chairs

- New and renovated facilities

- Technology

- Library materials

- Faculty development

- Student-faculty research

- New interdisciplinary programs

- Study abroad programs

If the institution wishes to increase the size of the faculty, presidents need to be able to communicate the value of adding positions to foster smaller class size, produce more favorable student-to-faculty ratios, and provide faculty with released time so they can supervise independent study and student research projects. They similarly need to explain how new and renovated facilities will enhance the education they provide. Perhaps most of all, they need to explain why the cost of providing students with an excellent education escalates more rapidly than the rate of inflation, describing, for example, the rapidly rising costs of technology and the pressure to increase financial aid in order to be competitive in attracting and retaining students.

As most fundraisers—presidential and others—know, successful fundraising is ultimately about making and keeping relationships. Effective fundraisers listen carefully to potential donors to discover what matters to them and then identify the synchronicity between the institution's needs and the donors' interests. This is especially important when donors are not attracted to any of the stated fundraising priorities. In such cases, presidents need to recognize that all money is fungible and that the paths to advancing their institution are multiple.

To be candid, what I most enjoyed about fundraising was working with donors to craft gifts that both animated them and benefited the college. One such moment came when I was walking on a beach in Japan with a trustee who was a Puget Sound graduate. I quickly learned that she had absolutely no interest in the gift that we had assumed she would favor: endowing a chair to honor her late father, who had been prime minister of Japan. She did, however, want to honor his commitment to Japanese-American understanding. By the end of our walk, the two of us had designed a program that would bring a Japanese student to study at Puget Sound every other year and in the alternate years would send one of our Asian studies graduates to Japan for an apprenticeship with an artist or a politician. She and her family quickly endowed this program with a very significant gift. The program has been tremendously successful.

Presidents also need to be able to refuse offered gifts that run counter to the institutional mission or are simply undesirable. An alumnus of a campus that was beautifully landscaped but landlocked wanted to build a gazebo in the center of campus so "the girls could have shelter from the rain." Apparently, he thought it was fine for the male students to get wet. For several years, the president unsuccessfully tried to persuade him to fund other projects. Then, when the college was building a new residence hall, it occurred to the president that the patio adjacent to the hall could be designed as a covered "half gazebo" or pergola. The architect provided some drawings. The alumnus fell in love with the idea and made a seven-figure bequest.

Of course, not all such stories end so happily. Sometimes presidents simply have to turn down well-intended gifts that please the donor but do not make institutional sense. Sometimes, colleges find themselves in the position of having to return a gift whose conditions they could not meet. For example, an Ivy League institution returned a $20 million donation to an alumnus who wanted to approve all faculty appointments that his money would make possible. The president, in my judgment, was right not to agree to this level of donor control. Others institutions have returned gifts and even taken donor names off buildings when it came to light that the individuals had been involved in illegal or immoral activity.

Principles of Fundraising

Although raising money is more art than science, here are some basic principles I encourage fundraising presidents to embrace.

First, it is important to remember that the gifts being solicited are not personal gifts to the president but rather gifts for something more important—the education of students and the support of a college or university about which most prospective donors care a great deal.

Next, knowledge about prospective donors matters. So does strategy. Thus, even before presidents try to establish a relationship with potential donors, they need to know as much about them as they can. In the best of all worlds, people already close to the institution, such as trustees, alumni, administrators, and faculty, know these prospects and can provide presidents and their staff with information about the interests, past philanthropy, and gift capacity of these prospects. They may be able to broker an introduction or ultimately join in the solicitation effort. The internet is also a rich source of information. Institutions also benefit from having on staff one or more researchers. Some colleges don't have the resources to hire their own researchers and so outsource the research.

Effective development staff members generally get to know potential donors and know that they are interested in making a major gift before bringing the president into the conversation. They should also have a good sense of the magnitude and purposes of the anticipated gift. Nevertheless, such collective wisdom may be mistaken, requiring presidents to be especially quick-witted. In one such moment, a president was sure that a longtime trustee was capable of giving a $5 million campaign gift. When, after careful cultivation, the president asked for a gift at this level, the donor laughed and said he couldn't possibly afford something of that magnitude. Worried that she might have offended him by asking, the president responded with a smile, "Well, aren't you flattered that I thought that you were?" In the end, the donor gave a $350,000 gift.

Furthermore, each donor needs to be cultivated in his or her own way. Many donors want (appropriately) to learn a great deal about the purpose of the gift before being solicited. If a proposed gift involves the academic programs, it makes sense for key faculty members to be brought into the conversations. If it is to be for financial aid, having donors meet with scholarship students—who can talk about the difference financial aid has made to their lives—can be extremely powerful. In contrast, some donors do not want extended contact before making a gift. They simply want to be involved in a conversation during which the president makes the case for a project and then follows up with a brief, one-page or two-page request and a budget. For example, one donor's representative urged a president who was asking for support for a library renovation: "Write a proposal of no more than a page and a half with a budget. Don't explain the importance of libraries. The donor knows that already. Just describe this particular project." A week later, a check for $1 million arrived in the mail. Another president tells a story about his first meeting with a major prospect. He had not planned to ask for a gift. Within fifteen minutes, the potential donor asked him, "Why are you here? How much money do you want and for what?" The president quickly came up with a seven-figure number and a project. The donor wrote the check within the week. (The president did wonder if he had left money on the table.)

Although there may be exceptions, it makes sense to include spouses or partners and sometimes children or parents when cultivating solicitations. An involved family member or partner, pleased at being included rather than ignored, can often become an important advocate.

Finally, presidents should never surprise a prospect by asking for a gift. Instead, they or members of their staffs should make it clear to potential donors whether a solicitation will take place. The solicitation usually does not occur until the president and prospect have developed a relationship. At that point, the president (or a staff member, if that makes more sense) should tell the potential donor the purpose of their meeting with the president. I suggest that when requesting a meeting at which the president plans to ask for a gift, the president explain directly, "I would like to meet with you to ask you for a gift. How would you like me to do that? Would you like your spouse or partner to be part of the conversation? Do you want me to come to your office or your home? Will it be OK with you if we first talk about a gift and I then follow up with a written proposal?" Such an approach means that the prospect will know the purpose of their meeting. This approach also eliminates awkwardness for presidents hoping to find the opportune moment to ask for the gift and for potential donors worrying about when the request will happen. If prospects tell the president not to bother meeting because they are not going to give a gift, their candor saves the president time and sometimes travel money. In every other case, by agreeing to the meeting the prospective donors have already made the decision that they will at least entertain a request.

Because many donors and presidents have developed social relationships and even friendships, I suggest that presidents separate the "business" part of their solicitation visit from the social. Thus, when presidents request a meeting, they might suggest that they and the prospective donor or donors first meet to talk about the gift and then, after that conversation, have lunch or dinner. Prospective donors then know that the request is for the purpose of the formal meeting but they will also have time later for purely social interaction. If the president's spouse or partner is available and interested, they should be included in the lunch or dinner.

Cultivating and Soliciting Trustees

The cultivation of board members should not only be a presidential priority but in many ways one of the president's most enjoyable responsibilities. If board members are truly informed about and engaged in the institution, they are more likely to provide it with generous financial support. There are, unfortunately, boards whose members do not believe it is their responsibility to contribute financially to the institution. One such trustee, a billionaire, told the president of the institution's foundation that if he were ever asked for a gift, he'd resign. He was a valuable board member for his time and his ideas. But he absolutely refused to write a check and finally did resign.

Based on their knowledge of their donor and alumni pools, presidents need to take the lead in identifying and cultivating future board members who are capable of making major gifts or providing important expertise. Current and former trustees, the development staff, and the alumni relations staff also can and should provide nominations. On some campuses, faculty members who have stayed in touch with graduates are eager to make suggestions.

Cultivating and Soliciting Alumni

When presidents visit a city to meet with an area alumni group, they should also try to share a meal either individually or in small groups with graduates who may become trustees or donors. These individuals are often flattered by the personal invitation and may be more likely to attend this more intimate event than a larger gathering.

Cultivating and Soliciting Parents

The population of current and former parents can be fruitful for both potential trustees and donors. Special parents' funds are often an important source of support. Parents with resources sometimes introduce themselves to the president at the orientation for new students and their families, making it clear in this initial conversation that they would like to support the institution financially. Other parents who are unable to make financial gifts may be pleased to volunteer.

One might assume that presidents would be cordial to everyone they meet, but the opposite occurred when one president met an affluent couple who had intended to give a gift to honor their son's graduation from a college they felt had served him well. Per their usual habit, they dressed casually for the commencement ceremony. Later, they stood in a long line to shake hands with the president, intending to hand him a very large check. The president was brusque, looking over their heads, apparently for more promising prospects. The couple held onto the check.

Cultivating and Soliciting Foundations

Presidents need to cultivate not only individuals but also private foundations, which are a wonderful source of support because they exist to give money away. Thus, whereas individuals need to be persuaded to give a gift, foundations simply need to be persuaded to give it to one particular institution for one particular project. At the same time, foundation officers should be cultivated and solicited in the same way individual donors are. Thus, presidents, at least annually and sometimes more often, should visit promising foundations in order to establish relationships with program officers and learn what the foundations are most interested in funding. These conversations also give presidents the opportunity to test out particular funding requests with the program officers, many of whom are very candid, and some of whom may even agree to read and make suggestions about draft proposals.

In turn, program officers are eager to talk to presidents to learn what they believe is important. In some instance, conversations with foundation officials will lead the foundation to fund something that was not on its list.

The process of seeking foundation funding is relatively straightforward. After reading the group's guidelines, presidents should make an appointment to visit, develop a relationship with the program officer or officers, and explore how their institution's needs might match the foundation's priorities. The institution then should draft a proposal, seeking the program officer's review, and submit the formal proposal.

Often an institution benefits if a member of the foundation board advocates for its proposal. For this reason, it makes sense for presidents to inform their trustees and influential alumni about which foundations they plan to solicit and provide them with a list of foundation board members whom the college's trustees and alumni would be willing to write or phone. At some foundations, such connections are necessary for them even to agree to consider an application.

Cultivating and Soliciting Corporations

The process for cultivating and soliciting corporations is similar to that for foundations, but at the earlier stages a senior development officer rather than the president might handle this process. Still, presidential involvement is likely to be necessary for those corporations that are responsive only to requests by someone at a high level in their organization or a member of their board. Corporations also tend to look more favorably on colleges from which they hire and projects that will benefit the local community.

Federal and State Funding

The federal and state governments have historically been sources of funding by way of grants, and in the case of the federal government, earmarks (which in the future may not persist). The process for seeking government grants is much the same as soliciting private foundations. Earmarks require good relationships between the college's president or trustees and members of Congress. Some institutions seek funding on their own, working directly with congressional staff. Others hire lobbyists, sometimes with great success. There are two important downsides to hiring lobbyists. First is cost, which can be significant and hard to justify if the funding is not forthcoming. Second, some lobbyists encourage colleges and universities to seek funding for initiatives that are not central to their mission simply because funding might be available for those initiatives.

Donor Stewardship

Whenever presidents meet with potential donors, they need to memorialize their meeting in notes, whether by dictating them, debriefing with a colleague, or sending emails to the development officer assigned to the prospects, with copies placed both in the advancement office and president's office files. These notes should not only document any requests for gifts and the response but also include any information pertinent to a gift or to the president's relationship with the prospective donors. Before meeting with those donors again, the president should review the notes in order to be able to refer back to the earlier conversations.

Donor stewardship should be standard practice. The president and staff members should routinely and periodically thank donors in person, by phone, and via email, describing the value that their gifts provided. Those who fund campus facilities should regularly be invited to attend events in those facilities. Those who fund lecture series or musical performances should be invited to dinner with the lecturers and the performers.

If gifts directly benefit individual students through scholarships or faculty members through endowed chairs, the beneficiaries should write personal thank-yous. Even better, the institution should arrange occasions where donors and recipients actually meet, perhaps over a lunch or dinner. An annual scholarship luncheon, for example, not only offers an opportunity for the donors and their beneficiaries to meet but also allows a student, faculty member, and donor to speak inspiringly about the importance of supporting the institution. Such interactions also inspire current students to decide to become contributing alumni.

Ultimately, whether presidents are ensuring that their institution uses its resources wisely and fairly or are raising money, they are most effective if they are able to articulate the institution's mission and their own vision for its future in compelling ways. They are even more effective if they can couple their more global perspective with an understanding of and appreciation for the institution's rich texture—its mix of talented faculty, staff, and students and its array of meaningful academic programs.

Of course, presidents play none of these roles privately. They are public figures. The next chapter will discuss how presidents and their spouses, partners, and families live life in a fishbowl.

5

Crafting a Private Life in a Public Context

One of the biggest challenges for college presidents is finding a way to create some semblance of a private life even as, by becoming a president, they have become public figures and renounced their anonymity, often no matter where they are in the world. For example, in a hotel lobby in Tokyo I found myself next to a friend of mine who was also a college president. On a Caribbean cruise, I ran into a former colleague and her family. And most strikingly, on a visit to the Royal Academy in London I happily encountered a Puget Sound alumna who, in order to fund her postgraduate year abroad, was working there. That night at the theater I was tapped on the shoulder by the couple seated behind me: the parents of a current Puget Sound student. The next afternoon, in Piccadilly Circus, I met a high school senior wearing a Puget Sound T-shirt whose uncle had given her a trip to London to celebrate her acceptance at Puget Sound for the coming fall.

Living in the Fishbowl

Public scrutiny of presidents extends to their private behavior and their personal relationships, which sometimes make their way into the popular press. In a number of highly publicized cases, presidents have been asked to resign because their boards deemed their behavior unbefitting.

One community college president, for example, gained national notoriety when a photograph surfaced of him on a boat appearing to pour beer from a keg into the mouth of a young woman. Although the president insisted that the keg was not open, it took his board only eight minutes to vote to ask for his resignation. In an interview reported in the local paper, a trustee said that after struggling with whether there should be a line between public and private behavior, the board decided that the president's personal life did matter because it shaped the public's perception of his job performance. Another president lost his job after he was arrested for a DUI—not once but twice in two days. Other presidents have lost their jobs for having affairs with a subordinate and for spending college funds for lavish vacations.

One would expect that someone who became a college president would have enough common sense to avoid flagrant behavior, but as Horace Greeley is reported to have said, "Common sense is very uncommon." Even so, my recommendations for presidents about their private behavior are fairly basic:

- To avoid attracting negative attention to themselves and their institution, presidents must always be conscious of how they and their board would react if accounts of their behavior were to appear on the front page of the newspaper, whether the local, national, or student paper.

- Presidents should heed an alter ego that constantly reminds them of the "need to be presidential"—that is, poised, calm, alert, articulate, and in control in all situations.

- Presidents should not assume that the power and influence they wield in their role as president will protect them if they abuse that power and influence.

- If a president is prone to becoming more garrulous or uninhibited after a drink or glass of wine, she or he should not drink in public or when representing the institution at private occasions.

- Under no circumstances should a president drink and drive.

- When in doubt about whether an expense should be charged to the institution, the president should not charge it or at the very least seek guidance from the board chair.

- If they find themselves in situations that might compromise the institution or themselves, presidents need to notify their board chair immediately.

The Importance of Appearance

Presidents are often assessed by their looks and dress. For example, throughout her very successful presidency at the University of Pennsylvania, Judith Rodin's dress and hairstyle were the subject of much public commentary. Molly O'Neill, a *New York Times* reporter, in an October 20, 1994 piece entitled "On Campus With: Dr. Judith Rodin: In an Ivy League of Her Own," described her this way: "In the gray-tweed and furrowed-brow world of academia, Dr. Rodin turns heads with her cover-girl smile and designer clothes." Almost nine years later, Daniel Duane, in "Eggheads United," a May 5, 2003 *New York Times* article about Rodin's stance toward unions, described her irrelevantly as having "her hair expertly frosted."

Writing about President Ruth Simmons receiving an award for her service as an educator at the BET Honors ceremony, a student blogger, Betsy Morais, a February 19, 2010 piece, "Presidential Fame Caucus: Ruth Simmons" that appeared in IvyGate, described Simmons as "looking absolutely radiant in a stunning and sexy black dress (64 and sexy? You show 'em, Ruth!).'" Gabriel Williams, writing for DRJAYS.com in a February 3, 2010 piece, "Celebrity Style: B.E.T. Honors 2010 Show," described President Simmons's appearance at that same event in a very different way: "Dr. Simmons wore a classic black evening dress with pearl accessories—very fitting and age appropriate."

Although the appearance of most male presidents escapes the attention of the press, former Harvard president Larry Summers and current Ohio State president Gordon Gee have not. Summers is frequently referred to "rumpled," as when Harvard student Brian Jacobs was quoted in a May 4, 2001 *Harvard Crimson* article, "The First Word on Larry Summers" by David Gellis. Jacobs said: "He was always rumpled—a bit the scatterbrained professor." Reporters as frequently comment about Gee's signature bow tie and his appearance generally. For example, in a July 12, 2007 piece in *USA Today*, "Ohio State Gets Popular Prez," Andrew Welsh-Huggens praised him for his "geeky" appearance: "Gee embodies the geeky college president. And right now geeky is in—along with a stellar fundraising portfolio and an affable manner."

More private stories about how presidents look abound. Trustees on the board of an institution that had benefitted from the president's accomplishments became concerned about the weight he had put on over the years. They anguished about whether they could suggest sending him to a weight-loss outpatient program; they decided not to. Another president was startled, on a Saturday afternoon, when she wore jeans to walk to the nearby grocery store, an alumna who happened to be in the checkout line in front of her chastised her for "appearing in public dressed like that." The alumna instructed this president that she should never go out in public unless she was wearing a skirt or dress, nylon stockings, and heels. The president chose to ignore her advice for Saturday afternoon walks to the grocery store, outdoor athletic events, and campus picnics. She was pleased when her students told her that they liked that she wore jeans to such events.

So how should presidents respond to such scrutiny? Most importantly, they simply need to be conscious that how they look will be a matter of interest not only to their campus colleagues but also to the community beyond. Thus, they need to think about the image they want to project on all occasions. Their safest choices: tailored clothes in subdued colors that travel well without wrinkling and do not call attention to their appearance other than by suggesting a professional persona.

Making Public Pronouncements

Most presidents learn very quickly that every word they utter in public and sometimes in private carries a weight that had not previously been the case. There is a real danger in this level of attention because it leads at least some presidents to believe that they do in fact have infinite wisdom, or at least thoughts and ideas worthy of significant attention. Too often in such cases presidents talk rather than listen, dominate conversations, and appear portentous. This often leads them to give overly long introductions to speakers when the audience, which more often than not has heard the president speak before, has come to hear the speaker.

Then there are those presidents who tend to give the same speech over and over again. The faculty at one university had heard the president's remarks at commencement so many times that they quietly began reciting them along with him. Because he was on a platform a fair distance from the faculty, he was unaware of the practice.

President Larry Summers of Harvard is perhaps the most notable example of a president who, in what he later characterized as an effort to be provocative in a private speech, created a firestorm of negative reaction that he apparently had not anticipated. In a January 14, 2005 presentation, "Remarks at NBER Conference on Diversifying the Science & Engineering Workforce," the transcript of which can be found on Harvard's Office of the President website, Summers posited that one reason why fewer women than men have successful careers in science and engineering is that they have innate differences in aptitude from men. His remarks received national and even international attention. Many commentators believe that this episode contributed to Summers's decision to leave the Harvard presidency.

There are also many examples of presidents who have intentionally and successfully used their position as bully pulpits in order to contribute to the public discourse. In such cases, if the matter is a controversial one, before speaking publicly, presidents will do well to consider a few points.

Despite all disclaimers to the contrary, listeners will assume that anything and everything presidents say is on behalf of their institution and not merely their personal opinion. Thus, in every instance, presidents need to weigh the costs as well as the benefits of their speaking out. I further recommend that when in doubt, don't.

When presidents speak out, it is prudent to do so about matters relating to higher education and their own institution. Specifically, they should avoid both endorsing political candidates and addressing controversial social issues that do not affect their campus. If they do choose to comment on potentially controversial matters, they should speak from a written text rather than in an impromptu fashion. They further should consult with trusted colleagues and their board chair about what they plan to say and how they will say it.

Finally, presidents need to anticipate public reaction to their opinions and be prepared with a carefully considered and carefully crafted response if that reaction occurs.

Living in an On-Campus President's House

Many presidents are required to live in a house on campus with the expectation that they will entertain there frequently. As one presidential spouse put it, "It's like living in the White House but without the Marine sentries." This arrangement can be both a blessing and a curse.

The positives of living on campus include proximity to the president's office, ease of attending campus events, and ability to entertain at a location convenient to the campus community. An on-campus house gives the president the opportunity to host special events, such as receptions for honor societies and guest speakers. Indeed, on most campuses, members of the campus community and especially students like to be invited to the president's house. I confess that sometimes requests to use the president's house can be a problem. For example, I was not amenable to a recent graduate's request that I make the house available for his wedding and reception. I suggested that the chapel, which was within sight of the house, would be a better location.

To find the right balance of public and private uses for the president's house, I suggest doing the following from the start.

Discuss with the board chair or the executive committee of the board the board's expectation for presidential on-campus entertaining and the resources, including staff, available for such entertaining.

Work with the president's cabinet to establish the principles governing which events the president will host, both at the house and elsewhere on campus, being mindful that hosting a certain kind of event will set a precedent. For example, if the president hosts an event for one group, other similar groups will wish to have the same done for them.

Ask the president's assistant to work with each of the vice presidents to propose a schedule of events at the house for the coming year, which the president should then review and perhaps revise.

Develop a protocol and assign responsibility for each kind of event. On some campuses, the president's spouse assumes this role and increasingly is paid for doing so. On other campuses, this role may be played by a staff member, such as a campus special events planner or, if there is one, the president's house manager. This person would in turn work with the appropriate people to design and implement the events. For example, for trustee events the president might work with the staff member who serves as secretary to the board; for alumni events he or she might work with the director of alumni affairs. This person might also, on the president's behalf, communicate to the campus catering service the president's expectations for the food and drink to be served at various occasions.

Finally, clarify expectations about how the president wants various events to be staffed. For example, most presidents will want to review a guest list with information about each guest no later than the day before the event. They might wish to have a staff person facilitate their conversations at events, ensuring both that they meet certain people and that no one person or group monopolizes their time. Because presidents cannot leave an event being held in their own home, they may want a staff member to make sure events end in a timely manner.

The negatives of living on campus are that the president has little if any privacy and never has the sense of being away from work. One new president, happily running on her treadmill at 7 A.M., was far from delighted when she was interrupted by a disgruntled faculty member who wanted to talk about an impending and controversial tenure decision. The president explained that it would be inappropriate for her to discuss the matter. Then, worried that she was being ungracious, she invited the faculty member in for coffee and a chat about other matters. There have also been acts of vandalism. One president became deeply concerned when, two years in a row, on the last night of spring semester classes, a rock was thrown through the house's first-floor picture window. Her first response was to consider setting up a system in which the moment someone walked on the grass close to the house, a recording of her voice would be activated, telling them to leave. She rejected that as impractical. She then considered a sprinkler system that would be similarly activated, but a colleague suggested that might provoke further vandalism. She eventually settled on installing lights around the house that were motion-activated. The problem ended.

I encourage presidents to consider purchasing an off-campus retreat for themselves, preferably close enough to campus that they will make use of it as they can but distant enough to give them a sense of quiet and privacy. Even if presidents do a great deal of work at this second home, being away from the center of campus life for the occasional few days can be revitalizing. Buying a home of their own also has a financial value because they might be able to build equity over time.

The Role of the Presidential Spouse or Partner

According to the 2007 American Council of Education's *American College Presidents Study*, most college presidents are married (89 percent of male presidents and 63 percent of female presidents). Thus, it is not surprising that even though it is illegal for search committees to ask about or consider marital status, most want to meet their finalists' spouses or partners.

In fact, when the departing president of the hiring institution is a man whose wife has devoted herself to playing the role of the campus's "first lady," at least one person on every presidential search committee with which I have worked has early in the process expressed the hope that the next presidential spouse will play the same supportive role. In every instance, someone else around the table, usually a woman, protested that the institution was hiring a president and not a spouse. This remark was often followed by an account of spouses (who often quickly became former spouses) who brought adverse publicity to the institution.

I always take this occasion first to remind committees that it is illegal for them to consider the marital status of their candidates. I then go on to describe some very successful presidents I know, both male and female, who either do not have a spouse, have a commuter marriage, have a spouse with a career of his or her own, or is in a committed relationship but unable to marry their same-sex partner. What has delighted me is that by the end of every search, committees have become receptive to a variety of different personal relationships for their next president.

Presidential spouses or partners may not always be an advantage. I know of several committees who have turned away from a candidate whom they greatly admired because of concerns about their spouse. In one such instance, I was told that the candidate's wife, throughout their campus visit, routinely interrupted her husband. The committee was concerned on two counts: they were put off by her behavior and they began to wonder about the candidate's ability to assert himself. In another situation where there was an internal candidate, several campus committee members shared with the entire committee their concerns about the spouse's ability to keep confidentiality. They provided examples. In a third situation, committee members were dismayed by the spouse's penchant for rudeness.

Of course, many spouses or partners add to a committee's enthusiasm about a potential president. One candidate in particular won the universal praise of a campus when he was asked, in an all-campus forum, an inappropriate question about the role his wife would play. Despite the inappropriateness, he responded that he would not presume to speak for his wife, who was in the audience, and so asked her if she would like to answer. She was articulate and gracious. He won points for not speaking for her; she won points for her presence of mind. He became the unanimous choice of the search committee and the board.

Search committees do need to understand that a spouse or partner is almost certainly going to influence the candidate's decision about taking the job if it is offered. Thus, the executive secretary to the search committee should make it a priority to work directly with the spouse or partner to arrange a schedule that responds to his or her interests. For example, spouses with school-age children will want to visit schools. Those who have careers often hope to meet people in their profession. Yet others will be interested in volunteering or have hobbies and want to get to know people who share those interests. The same, by the way, is true for school-age children who have particular extracurricular passions. I know of several candidates whose children were persuaded that a move they dreaded would be positive when, accompanying their parents on the campus visit, they met other children their age and learned about opportunities to pursue their interests.

Just as it is critical for the president and the board to have clear expectations of one another, it is as essential that the spouse or partner is clear about the role she or he wishes to play on campus and understands whether that role is in fact a feasible one. For example, if the spouse or partner hopes to be employed by the institution in a role other than supporting the president, such as teaching or serving on the staff, the institution needs to decide and communicate what will be possible. If the agreement is that the only role for the spouse or partner will be to play a supporting role to the president, then the board chair needs to define the expectations for that position, whether it will be a paid position, and if so at what level. Whether the spouse or partner is employed or not, it is also helpful for him or her to know what institutional support will be available, which expenses will be reimbursed, and whether and to what extent their travel with the president will be funded.

The president's partner or spouse will be living in the same fishbowl as the president and subject to the same scrutiny. Thus, a president's wife who was critical of the town in which the university was located created problems for her husband as well as for herself. In contrast, the husband, who was an asset at alumni events and with donors and who served as an informal mentor to lots of students, won the affection of the campus.

Finally, most presidents thrive on the interaction they have with members of the campus community when they attend events. Indeed, sitting with and getting to know students or colleagues can be one of the most positive aspects of such events. But I have known presidential spouses who have felt that interaction to be an intrusion on their private time. Here too some clarity from the beginning: the knowledge that whenever presidents are in public they are working can help their spouses make their own adjustment to their public role.

The Single President

When the presidential search committee at Puget Sound asked me what I would need in order to say yes to an offer to become president, I unhesitatingly (and almost unthinkingly) said, "A surrogate wife." I had been divorced for seventeen years. My daughter was a junior in college. After the laughter subsided, I explained my reasoning: I would not be able to be an effective president and also arrange for all the entertaining I anticipated doing, not to mention managing an eighty-five-hundred-square-foot house. The board wound up hiring a live-in house manager who was terrific and freed me to focus on being president.

When I attended the Harvard Seminar for New Presidents the week after I took office, I was especially interested in the evening session for those of us who were, at least at the time, unmarried. Of the six of us (out of a class of approximately forty-five) who were single, five were women. The only man in the group was a priest. Our teachers stressed the point I made at the beginning of this chapter: presidents essentially have no private lives. They advised us that whether it was fair or not, because we were single our personal lives were likely to receive extra scrutiny. To avoid generating gossip, they advised us to be discreet at all times. For example, they urged us when entertaining "to keep the blinds down" and to show up in public with a date only if we were certain the relationship was leading to marriage.

One member of this group decided at some point during the subsequent year that she did want to get married. Brave woman that she was, she told her board in closed session that she wanted them to introduce interesting single men to her so that she could find a husband. Some of the trustees did so, and as far as I know, she has been happily married since then. In my case, I followed the advice to keep my blinds down and any personal relationships private until I surprised the campus midway through my first year by marrying someone I had known but was not dating when I became a candidate for and then was offered the presidency.

Probably the biggest burden for a single president is the lack of a trusted partner with whom to share the highs and lows and even the moments of uncertainty that inevitably are part of every presidency. Indeed, it makes sense for all presidents, whether single or in a relationship, to have coaches, mentors, and friends whom they trust and with whom they talk regularly.

Discretion and Humor

Although the conversation I described earlier at the Harvard Seminar for New Presidents, about the need for single presidents to be particularly cautious, occurred in 1992, and although social mores have changed substantially since then, I continue to believe that it makes sense for all presidents to exercise discretion. As one former president put it: "Presidents live under the microscope of somebody's curiosity."

But no matter how discreet and appropriately behaved, presidents remain subject to an amazing array of rumors that have no grounding in fact whatsoever. I know of presidents who have been the object of scurrilous and untrue reports about their personal behavior. Others have been described as being on the job market when they are not and as having health problems when they do not. In such instances, I urge presidents to discuss such rumors with their board chair, and if the chair so advises with other trustees, and also with the members of the president's cabinet so that people in leadership positions will not be surprised by the rumors and are able to counter them. And if possible, president should try privately to deflect such rumors with humor. For example, one president—a divorced woman—responded to rumors about her personal life, "If only a fraction of those rumors were true, I'd be having much more fun than I am having now." Because the rumor-mongers were unable to get a rise out of her, they eventually ceased spreading untrue stories.

Although others may disagree, I advise presidents not to dignify rumors with a public response, if only because responding keeps the stories alive. A public response may also attract media attention, which would give the rumors broader currency than they would otherwise have. I suggest instead that presidents focus on the importance of their work and how it has almost certainly enriched their lives and always behave in public with as much grace and graciousness as they can muster.

Ultimately, presidents occupy a space that can be as public as that of a politician but, unlike politicians, presidents serve at the pleasure of their board, not that of the voting citizenry. Unlike politicians, they are not judged by their positions on social, economic, and military issues or on achieving broad popularity. Indeed, wise presidents avoid making pronouncements on such issues because they understand that what they say will inevitably be read as articulating the institution's position. Finally, college presidents, while living in a fishbowl, are both selected and reappointed based not on their popularity but on their expertise, their abilities, and their effectiveness in accomplishing their stated goals. Sadly, this is often not the case for politicians.

6

Letting Go and Leaving Gracefully

College presidencies almost always begin with great optimism, a sense of possibilities to be realized. In many cases, that optimism is merited, and the presidency ends with a well-deserved celebration of accomplishments. Other presidencies end simply because the president has decided that it is time to retire, for family reasons, or because she or he has moved on to another position. Yet others end with disappointment and anger on the part of all parties.

In the best circumstances, presidential transitions are relatively seamless. Many presidents who are leaving for another position inevitably turn their attention to their new life, leaving the proverbial open field for the next president. Some retiring presidents are so comfortable with themselves and with what they have achieved that they quite happily turn the institution over to their successor. Some do more: they go out of their way to be helpful to the new president, introducing her or him to donors, providing insights into trustees and faculty, and just talking enthusiastically to anyone who will listen about how the institution is going to be in great hands.

Once an appointment is made, the outgoing president ideally plays an important role in the transition, ensuring that the president-elect receives as much information as possible about the institution. If the outgoing president is leaving under unfavorable circumstances or for some other reason is unable to shepherd the transition process, the board chair may wish either to ask one of the vice presidents or name a transition committee (perhaps a few members from the search committee) to play that role. In these cases, the outgoing president needs to distance her- or himself from the process. If this president does not do so voluntarily, the board chair again needs to intervene.

Letting Go

Some outgoing presidents find it very difficult to let go. Inevitably, the longer their tenure, the more likely they will feel a good deal of ambivalence about leaving a role that has been a critical part of their identity. The wives of several retiring long-term presidents have confided their fear that their husbands will not know what to do with themselves because the institution had been their entire life. And several retiring presidents have described themselves as being in mourning over leaving a way of life that they loved so much.

Creating Problems for Presidents-Elect

Although it is understandably hard to let go, if presidents fail to leave gracefully, they create problems for their successors, and in a number of instances, tarnish their own legacy. A few examples are instructive:

- One retiring president was so determined that the college continue to fulfill his agenda that in the fall of his last year—without the board's knowledge, much less their approval—he commissioned a campaign case study that laid out his vision for the future and a set of fundraising priorities. The case study featured him prominently. There was no mention at all of an impending presidential transition.

The day after his successor's appointment was announced, the college's vice president for advancement called the president-elect to tell her that the case statement was "in bluelines" and ready to go to press. The vice president asked his new boss-to-be if she wanted to see the text before it went to the printer. The call startled the president-elect because she and the board had already agreed that the college would not begin planning a campaign until her second year. She responded: "What case statement? What campaign?" She asked the vice president to send her the document and not to send it to the printer before hearing from the board chair about next steps. She immediately called the board chair, who shared her surprise and stopped the process. Despite the board chair's intervention, it was an awkward moment for the president-elect. Her predecessor never mentioned this episode to her, nor did she raise it with him or anyone else. Two years later, after a strategic planning process, the board approved the new president's recommended slate of fundraising goals. These were, in significant ways, different from those favored by the now former president.

- Something similar happened when on outgoing president thought that in his final year he could and should set the institutional agenda for the coming decade. He persuaded himself that doing so would serve the university and be helpful to his successor. He argued that having a clear agenda would enable the search committee to focus on hiring a new president who would subscribe to it. He then moved energetically to establish a strategic planning process. He began to talk about the need for the university to redefine its mission in the face of new external realities. He contemplated launching the quiet phase of a new fundraising campaign. He commissioned a branding study. His vice presidents and a great many faculty members questioned the timing of all of these efforts, privately telling one another that they thought such activities should be the province of their next president. All of this was happening without board involvement. In fact, the trustees had agreed that they wanted their next president to be visionary and entrepreneurial. They were clear that they would look to him or her to lead a new strategic planning process, which would determine the next iteration of fundraising goals. The inevitable collision occurred. The result: the board chair told the retiring president, with whom he had worked very closely and admired for many years, that he was to cease and desist all such efforts. The president chose to respond graciously, telling the campus that on reflection he had decided that the planning process should indeed await his successor. He also praised the work the campus had done to date on planning, positing that it would provide the next president with a platform from which to launch a new planning process.

- Another retiring president so regretted that he had resigned after nearly thirty years in office that even as a national and widely publicized search for his successor was under way, he began confiding in people that he hoped that the board would dissuade him from leaving. What he did not realize was that even though the trustees and the campus had great respect and affection for him, they were eager for new leadership and new ideas. As one faculty member told the search consultant, "This time around we really do need a president who knows how to use email and voicemail."

- A second retiring president who regretted that decision went to his board on the eve of the campus visit of the first of three finalists who had been selected by the search committee after a national search. In this case, the board decided to keep him on and cancelled the search. I have no idea how the campus at large responded to this circumstance.

Creating Problems for Senior Staff

Outgoing presidents need to remember that many members of the senior staff are likely to have significant anxiety about the transition. Each, after all, serves at the pleasure of the president, and so they inevitably have questions about whether the next president will want them to continue. They all know stories of new presidents who immediately "clean house" in order to bring in their own team.

This is a case where communication between the incumbent president and the board chair is important. For example, if the board is not looking for the next president to make significant changes, the incumbent president—by his or her outward calm about the search and expressions of belief that the next president will value talent—can calm anxiety.

I also know of a number of instances when the board chair has met individually with the vice presidents, telling them that he or she hoped they would remain for at least the first year of the new president's tenure, both to determine if the fit was right for them and to assist in the transition.

Outgoing presidents should not take as their model the president who—despite his board's expressed confidence in the senior staff—irresponsibly alarmed his closest colleagues by telling them that they would be vulnerable, because the new president would almost certainly want to constitute his or her own team. He believed that he was appropriately cautioning them that their world was going to change. The vice presidents then shared their worries with the search consultant, who turned to the board chair. The board chair tried to reassure the vice presidents by meeting individually with each of them to thank them for their excellent work. She made no reference to the president's negative comments, but her conversations relieved their anxiety.

Some outgoing presidents have, unfortunately, put the members of their senior staff in a difficult position during the transition. An extreme example was the long-term president who instructed his cabinet members not to talk to the president-elect without his permission. He also demanded a report after each such conversation. The president-elect was wise enough to back off from conversations with the people who would soon be reporting to him, not wanting to put them in a strained position. What the outgoing president hadn't recognized was "the king is dead; long live the king" phenomenon, which meant that on the first day of the incoming president's tenure, the outgoing president would be, as students say, "history."

Once in office, the new president gently reminded his new colleagues that their need to observe confidentiality about many institutional matters extended to the former president. The result: the retiree was cut off from the campus in a way that probably would not have happened had he been more welcoming of the new "king."

The most extreme example of a president not letting go, however, is surely the former president who in the first year of his successor's tenure gave an interview to the local press criticizing what was, admittedly, a controversial presidential action. The new president remained publicly gracious to the retiree and continued to invite him to appropriate campus events, but ended the monthly lunches the two had enjoyed and no longer seated the former president at the head table at any event.

The President's House

Just as the president's house can be a problem for incoming presidents, so it can be for outgoing presidents. One president refused to allow the finalists for his position to see the house. Only when the board chair intervened did he reluctantly allow them and their spouses to have a tour. His reluctance to cooperate with the search created a certain awkwardness with his successor, an awkwardness that would not have been there if had been gracious about opening up what was, in fact, not his private home but the home where the institution required its presidents to reside.

There are also cases of former presidents who, upon retirement and to the dismay of their successors, immediately buy a house in the same neighborhood as the president's house. One of the incoming presidents was so unhappy with this situation that he persuaded the trustees to allow him to live elsewhere.

Involvement in the Search

Some retiring presidents hope to choose their own successor, something most search consultants and boards discourage for several reasons. First, choosing the president is the board's responsibility. Second, if the new president fails, the retiring president will be blamed for the selection, something likely to overshadow the positive aspects of his or her legacy. Finally, when outgoing presidents recruit candidates, they may inadvertently give those individuals the mistaken sense that they have favored status.

The Role of the Board Chair

Reluctant retirees make the board chair's job a delicate one. Often, the relationship between the board chair and the president has been a close and positive one, and the board chair wants the retiree to leave feeling valued. At the same time, the chair must be mindful that it is even more important that the incoming president be treated appropriately.

As soon as possible after the announcement that the president will be leaving, the board chair should be clear about the role that he or she should play both during the search and after an appointment is made. In the likely event that the outgoing president will not be involved in the search, the search committee chair should explicitly tell committee members that their pledge of confidentiality about the search extends to the president. The chair might also add that she or he will be the only person to discuss the search in any way with the president. The chair should make it clear that the president understands and agrees with this approach. This can sometimes be awkward, particularly if a member of the president's office serves as staff to the search committee, which is often the case. This will be the first time in a president's tenure not to possess important information, but it is a good time to start the process of letting go by quietly keeping a distance from the search.

Finalists usually want to meet with the outgoing president, to ask questions and learn what the outgoing president thinks are the campus's important challenges and opportunities. Because most presidents want a successor who will build on their accomplishments, such conversations give them the opportunity to sell the institution to candidates. It also sets the stage for their future relationship.

Even when the outgoing president is not a formal part of the interview process, the board or search committee chair is likely to ask the president for a confidential assessment of the finalists. In this case, the outgoing president should be candid but also prepared that the committee may come to a very different assessment. But besides having this conversation with the committee chair, or when the chair does not solicit the president's opinion, the outgoing president needs to keep quiet—not only during the search but forever after.

Leaving Gracefully

Outgoing presidents can do a great deal to effect a successful transition.

First, presidents might ask each member of the cabinet to draft an analysis of each of their areas for the eyes of only the president-elect, focusing on the area's strengths, opportunities, and challenges as well as any resource needs. Such analyses might also contain recommendations for how the new president might productively support or be involved in ongoing initiatives. By making their successor the audience for these analyses, outgoing presidents give their senior colleagues the powerful signal that they understand that the world is going to change and that they are fine with and even welcome those changes.

They would be wise to use the occasion of retirement to cele-brate the institution rather than themselves. Although campuses will want to honor retiring presidents who have had successful tenures, presidents can turn such occasions into celebrations of the strengths of the institution and the work of the faculty, staff, and students.

Even if presidents and advancement staff members have been diligent about creating reports of contacts with donors, presidents might consider carrying a handheld recorder for a time, recording whenever there is time what is known about major donors. A staff member could transcribe these notes for the president-elect.

During the transition, departing presidents might offer to ac-company their successor on purely social visits to donors, founda-tions, corporations, and as appropriate, state and federal officials to make introductions and give the world the signal that the outgoing president fully supports the incoming one. Incoming presidents can make it clear to those whom they meet that they will return for a more formal conversation once they are in office.

One particularly gracious outgoing president learned that her students especially valued the way that she had involved herself in what they themselves referred to as their "quirky traditions." She thus made it a point to invite the president-elect soon after being appointed to join her and play the central role in one of the traditional events. The students and the president-elect were delighted.

What Incoming Presidents Need to Know

Perhaps most of all, incoming presidents benefit from gaining an understanding of the campus culture and any of its idiosyncrasies. They also benefit from understanding the history behind any on-going critical issues, any political land mines, and the campus's expectations generally of its next president. I recommend that the incoming presidents ask their predecessor questions like these:

- If the outgoing president were not retiring but staying for another three to five years, what would his or her priorities be?

- What does the president see as the biggest challenges facing the institution in the short and long terms? What does the president see as the institution's greatest opportunities in the short and long terms?

- If the outgoing president could redo decisions or actions, what would those be in relationship to the faculty, students, staff, trustees, alumni, and the community?

- How does the outgoing president allocate time? What percentage of time does she or he spend on campus versus away from campus? Is that the right balance?

- What are the expectations of the campus in terms of presidential visibility? Do those expectations seem appropriate, or is the occasion of a new president a time to try to revise them?

- If the campus were suddenly to receive an unexpected and unrestricted gift of a million dollars, for what purposes would the president dedicate these funds and why? What contingency funds does the institution have? If the institution faced an unexpected and significant financial shortfall, what would the outgoing president recommend might be cut and why?

- What is likely to be the new president's biggest surprise?

- How does the campus define and practice shared governance?

- Is there a clear understanding both on campus and among the trustees of who is responsible for what?

- Do administrative offices work well together and think institutionally or do staff members focus primarily on their own area? What operational role do academic departments and program chairs play?

- Finally, do members of the faculty interact regularly and productively with colleagues from other disciplines or programs? And do members of the faculty interact regularly and productively with staff members?

So What Should Retired Presidents Do?

Probably the first thing that retired college presidents should do is separate themselves, at least for some time, from the institution they led. This not only gives their successors the opportunity to establish themselves, free from their predecessor's shadow, but also forces the retirees to accept the reality that their identity is no longer being a college president and that the rhythms of their life are no longer that of the academic calendar.

I encourage new retirees for at least a year and probably more not to subscribe to the student newspaper, read board materials, or—most of all—talk to anyone on campus other than their successor about institutional matters, and only then when the successor initiates the conversations. Even when, as in my case, the institution is doing incredibly well, it is hard for retiring presidents to let go of worrying. My daughter was a huge help in this regard, telling me again and again, "Mom, repeat after me: 'It's not my problem.'"

Because presidencies are so demanding, outside of their families most presidents have devoted themselves to their work. Indeed, every activity of most presidents is related in one way or another to their presidency. For example, if presidents serve on nonprofit boards in their own communities and on state and national educational boards, they usually do so by virtue of their office. Most of their social interactions relate to their work. Often they are able to read only work-related materials. It should not be a surprise, then, that many retiring presidents, after having no personal time, aren't sure what to do with their new abundance of it.

Unless they have already identified new pursuits, I suggest that retirees give themselves at least six months before committing to any new time-consuming projects. Several have confided that they devoted these first six months to catching up on sleep. Others took this time to develop a personal strategic plan that was comprehensive in nature, taking into account time with family and friends, possible professional pursuits, volunteer work, and hobbies. As one put it, "I once again have to decide who I want to be when I grow up."

There are wonderful examples of presidents who have reinvented themselves—going on to serve as officers of private foundations, heading various higher education associations, serving as consultants, writing books, speaking extensively about matters related to higher education. Some return to their roots, teaching and writing again in their academic specialties. Some serve as interim presidents. At least one former president has founded a nonprofit foundation to help disadvantaged youngsters. Many serve actively on nonprofit boards; some become active in social causes. Some even change their minds about retirement and after a time assume a new presidency.

Most presidents have come to love the institution they have served. Their sorrow at leaving is genuine. Those around them should try to understand the difficulty they may have in letting go. At the same time, those who have been closest to the president—whether trustees, members of the senior staff, or faculty leaders—serve both their president and the institution well by helping them understand that the best gift they can give the college or university they love is to transfer its leadership to someone new—and then gracefully move on.

7

The Pleasures of the Presidency

Despite the unrelenting demands on a president's time, energy, and psyche, the job brings with it extraordinary pleasures. To balance the challenges described in earlier chapters, in this chapter I relate stories I was told by a number of current and former presidents who described what it was about the job that brought them genuine happiness. To their stories, I have taken the liberty of adding a few of my own.

Although the details differ, each of these presidents talked about how important they felt it was to make a difference in their students' lives. Most talked as well about the pleasure of facilitating and celebrating the work of the faculty and improving the quality and reputation of their institution. Several mentioned the pleasure of working closely with staff members. Others highlighted their relationship with trustees. Many described their elation at securing major gifts and grants.

Many presidents take special pleasure in having the ability that only a president has to make things happen. As one president put it, "Exhilaration best describes presidents' emotions as they are often at the center of the swirl of ideas, accomplishments, issues, and controversies. The pleasure of being president has a great deal to do with assisting in the accomplishments and fulfillment of the hopes and expectations of others."

Another president, in his second presidency, finds his greatest pleasure in "taking care of an institution that I genuinely love and totally believe in, and positioning it for a brighter future." He is especially drawn "to problems and issues that have an exceptionally *long* time frame, where decisions my colleagues and I make today will reverberate for decades" because he recognizes that "at every place I've been, I feel that I am the beneficiary of smart decisions made by my predecessors." His story about the wisdom of one of his predecessors in creating an arboretum made me think about R. Franklin Thompson, an earlier Puget Sound president who during his tenure from 1942 to 1973 asked donors unable or unwilling to make a major gift at least to fund planting a tree. Many did. Today, Puget Sound's one-hundred-acre campus is quite spectacular, in great part because of the trees that not only form an arboretum but also meander throughout the campus.

A president in his fourteenth year of successfully leading a public university quantified the pleasure he receives in his work against the pain it causes him: "I have an 80/20 principle that I share with new presidents. I'll tolerate 20 percent in order to do the 80 percent that I love. There are times when the 20 percent may occupy 100 percent of my life for a week or even a month or so but, on balance, this 80/20 ratio continues to hold. It's why I continue to get great pleasure out of being president."

Perhaps the most moving comment came from a highly successful president who had over his several decades in office transformed two institutions in significant ways. He explained that leading these transformations and helping prepare students to be contributing citizens and lead satisfying personal lives was "a blessing, a gift from God, for which those of us who [have] made a difference as president should light candles."

The Students

Sara Lipka, in a November 28, 2010 *Chronicle of Higher Education* piece titled "New President Gamely Honeymoons with Carleton," described how Carleton's new president, Steven G. Poskanzer, earned the admiration of students and a trustee by wholeheartedly participating in a student prank that involved a campus icon—the plaster bust of Johann Christoph Friedrich von Schiller. Poskanzer carried Schiller's bust around with him when he was shaving or having dinner, for example, photographing their "interactions" and then posting them on the college's Facebook page. After reading the *Chronicle* piece, a former liberal arts college president observed, "This story illustrates precisely why being a college president is so enormously attractive to folks who treasure interaction with bright and quirky undergraduates."

Such interactions are the high points of many presidencies, as the following stories indicate:

- The president of a public university reminisced about her daily walks with her little dog across the campus, early in the morning, at lunchtime, or in the evening. The dog, she said, "gave me an easy way to strike up a conversation with students, and what wonderful conversations we had! Sometimes it was about their personal life; sometimes they wanted to tell me about a professor they particularly enjoyed. On days when I was having a particularly intense day, I would just step out of my office and walk over to the cafeteria or into a classroom; seeing the students interacting always reminded me what business I was in, why I was putting up with difficult personnel or budget decisions, etc."

- The president of a predominantly commuter campus made it a practice to stand in the center of campus every Friday morning, tossing a football with students on their way to and from class, something they all enjoyed. His students set up a Facebook page, celebrating that he actually knew their names.

- A first-year president of a small college set up a study table on weeknights at the president's house, complete with refreshments. He delighted in talking with the students.

- The now-retired president of a national liberal arts college from time to time showed up in the library at midnight, inviting students to go out for pizza with him. It was hard to know who was more enthusiastic about these excursions: he or the students. His alumni still tell stories about their pizza with the president.

- The president of another liberal art college from time to time wandered around the library late in the evening handing out cookies to students studying there.

- A president who had a reputation for a zany sense of humor delighted students (and himself) by occasionally rolling a bowling ball down the main hallway outside his office.

- The president of a public university institution with army, navy, and marine ROTC programs took "great pride in seeing the eager and confident faces [of the newly commissioned officers who might well be sent to Iraq or Afghanistan], knowing that the institution I led prepared these young people to serve our nation in critical leadership roles."

- Many presidents detailed their pleasure at witnessing how proud the families of the graduates were and how exuberant the graduates were. One noted the special joy she felt at giving diplomas to the graduates who were children of staff members. The graduates, many of them who might not otherwise have been able to afford college, benefited from the tuition waiver for children of employees.

Most presidents particularly cherish those moments when they hear from graduates of earlier years to thank them for their education.

- A former president of a historically black college put it this way, "The president's greatest pleasure will come not immediately but years after when you receive a letter from a former student who informs you that he/she is currently serving in a high-ranking post in the United States government and gives you thanks for all that you did to raise the academic standards at the university, make all people (regardless of religion or race) feel welcome, and who ends by thanking you for opening his eyes to the possibilities that were beyond the university's walls."

- The retired president of a comprehensive university cherishes the Facebook posting from one student who wrote: "You are my mentor, and I don't think I would have gotten my bachelor and master's degree without knowing and being inspired by you."

- One of Puget Sound's graduating seniors, the aptly named Sunshine Morrison, by her eloquent explanation on two occasions about what a Puget Sound education had done for her, moved me beyond measure. First, she joined me in speaking at a national conference. She told this large audience that because the faculty knew her as an individual and cared about her intellectual growth, she challenged herself and achieved more than she would have otherwise. She further noted that because the faculty respected her, she had become truly accountable for her own learning. A year after she graduated, Sunshine wrote the following memorable letter: "I will always cherish the four years that I spent at [Puget Sound]. It is there that I was challenged in ways I never thought possible, learned to fear any class that ended in the suffix 'ology,' made lifelong friends, found mentors in caring and dedicated faculty members, became a community coordinator, learned that calculus can actually be (dare I admit) fun, fell in love . . . had my heart broken, was inspired to pursue my MBA and in a day that will live forever in my family's collective memory—graduated from college."

There are also presidents who were graduates of the institution they now lead. Two of them have said that their greatest pleasure was in coming back home to their alma mater to become president. They saw themselves as coming back to a college they loved with the opportunity to make it even better. In both cases, many of the trustees with whom they worked had been their classmates, which gave them a bond of shared memories and shared devotion to their institution.

Dedicated Staff and Faculty

It is common on college campuses for members of the staff and faculty to give generously of their time and their talent, routinely accomplishing more than their jobs require in ways that matter enormously to a student or a group of students. When such generous actions happen frequently, they become part of the fabric of the institution and shape its general ambience. Effective presidents, more than anyone else on the campus, know about these contributions, often hearing stories about such individuals from members of the campus community, parents, and alumni.

Presidents have told with pride about the cook who routinely made chicken soup from scratch for students who were sick, the custodian who daily placed home-grown flowers in the entrance hallway of the administration building, the cashier who knew and remembered the name of every student who came through the cafeteria line, the secretaries who mentored their work-study students, the faculty member who served as scorekeeper for the basketball teams, and the executive vice president who pinch-hit as the golf coach when there was an unexpected vacancy in that position.

Here are a few other stories about how working with the faculty and staff gave presidents pleasure:

- The president of a large community college was especially passionate about the difference his work made to the faculty:

"Some of my greatest pleasures involved seeing the success of others, including a faculty-developed honors program in the humanities that included internships at the Smithsonian Institution and study abroad, and a privately funded honors business program that included bringing nationally known business leaders to campus."

- A president who was struggling with a micromanaging board found solace in her work with the custodians and groundspeople, whom she identified as "the most important work group on campus." She also explained that they are "the first-line people who tell the public" who and what the president is.

- Commencement is a time when presidents are vividly reminded of the importance of their work, especially when students and their parents tell stories about how certain professors made a huge difference in the students' lives. They often hear stories about how many faculty members, without additional compensation, advised students on independent study and summer research projects; devoted time and energy to counseling them about study abroad programs, fellowship applications, graduate school, and careers; attended performances and athletic events in which their students participated; and wrote lots of letters of recommendation. One very enthusiastic parent, thrilled that her son had won a major postgraduate fellowship in the sciences, exclaimed, "We always knew Benjy was smart, but today he is a scientist!"

- I have often witnessed the generosity of colleagues, but the moment that stands out for me came some months after a terrible ice storm had destroyed literally hundreds of trees throughout Puget Sound's tree-lined campus. Without telling anyone, members of the grounds crew cured the wood of the largest tree that had fallen and then built an oversized picnic table that they placed in what was known as "The President's

Woods." Once the table was in place, they showed up at my office and asked me to come with them for a surprise. Resonating with my mantra about the importance of creating inviting spaces for conversation, they had decided to have something positive come out of that devastating storm. The outcome was indeed positive: students and faculty made great use of that table and eventually the area was dubbed "the outdoor classroom."

- Several presidents host and especially enjoy thank-you events for the faculty and staff. On several campuses, these take the form of a picnic for employees and their families. On at least one campus, the president hosts an annual staff luncheon that is catered by an outside company so that the foodservice staff can attend. Faculty volunteers serve the food. In the summer, one president treats members of the campus community and their families to a minor league baseball game and picnic at the area ballpark as a way of saying thank you.

Fundraising

Gifts and grants, of course, always occasion great happiness for presidents because they often allow the institution to do something it otherwise would not be able to do. As one president noted after securing his college's first gift of more than $1 million, "Getting the gift was a heady experience, but the true joy was in sharing the excitement of faculty and students as they celebrated their new opportunities."

Presidents also come to understand that making a gift brings the donors great pleasure. One such donor had grown up riding his bike on the college campus, imagining himself as a student there. After serving four years in the marines, he was able to enroll, thanks to the GI Bill. When decades later he sold his business for

$10 million, he gave the college $2 million. Like so many other major donors, he declared that the moment of giving was one of the happiest of his life.

Donors and presidents also experience great joy when they witness the fruits of particular gifts—for example, when they meet with students who are able to thrive academically because of scholarships they have endowed, get to know faculty members whose accomplishments as teachers and scholars were supported by endowed chairs or faculty development programs that they have funded, see the positive impact their support for student-faculty research made on both the students and faculty involved, and recognize that their contributions to renovation and new construction is manifest not only in the bricks and mortar but in the difference those projects make in the life of the campus. I should stress that the presidents who most experience these pleasures are those who have developed close, personal relationships with both the donors and those on campus who will benefit from the gifts.

Making Things Happen

Perhaps the greatest pleasure for a president is in being able to make things happen in ways that only a president can, although in every instance wise presidents immediately acknowledge that most of what they got done was because of the good work of faculty and staff colleagues, trustees, and donors. The president of a multicampus community college system, for example, found pleasure in collaborating with the faculty who previously had a history of contentiousness with the administration. But his greatest pleasure came when, on his retirement, the faculty union formally recognized him for working on behalf of students, saying that he was "one of a kind."

Nevertheless, even as presidents rely on collaboration, a great many things on their campus would not happen without their making particular decisions. What follows is just a sampling of what presidents have done:

- Presidents have made improvements to the campus in ways that transformed campus life. Some presidents, for example, moved all parking and roadways to the periphery of the campus, creating a pedestrian and park-like setting that improved admissions, retention, and morale. Others secured private gifts or state funding for significant new academic buildings, residence halls, student centers, and recreational areas.

- Presidents have enabled the faculty to develop new programs. Over twenty years one president created six new colleges and an honors program that significantly enhanced the institution, its quality, and its reputation. Others have provided the impetus for successful new interdisciplinary programs, revised core curricula, and new graduate programs.

- They have dramatically increased enrollment and either maintained or enhanced student quality.

- They have deliberately decreased the size of their student body in order to "right-size" the campus, improve the student-faculty ratio, and enhance student quality.

- They have created strategic partnerships with their boards. One president twenty years later still remembers the moment early in his presidency when a divided board that included many senior members who were resistant to change came together in support of his vision for the future. At that moment, this president recognized that he had earned the board's trust and would now be able to play a leadership role.

- They have championed one of more of the following initiatives that made a positive difference on their campuses: living-learning communities; civic engagement, community service, and service learning; sustainability on their own campuses and beyond; greater opportunities for study abroad; a more diverse campus community.

I sometimes tell presidential candidates that I am glad that when I took my own presidency, I was naive. Had I known then what I now know about some of the challenges I would face, I might never have taken the job. Yet I'm glad that I did take it because the work was unquestionably the most satisfying of my life.

What is the lesson from all of this? To be both effective and happy, college presidents need most of all to be passionate about wanting to make a difference for students, the faculty, and the institution generally. They need to believe in the importance of the academic enterprise. They need to embrace their institution's mission. They also need to enjoy being on a college campus and view many of their responsibilities as benefits, such as attending student performances, art exhibits, and athletic events. They need to be genuinely interested in the work of the faculty and the life of the mind. They need to enjoy getting to know and interact with alumni. They need to want to be partners with the local community. They need to forge a relationship of mutual respect and support with their board.

Presidents also need to have a high tolerance for campus politics. They need to be able to listen to but not be devastated by criticism. They need the capacity and the willingness to make timely and difficult decisions. They need to appreciate the vagaries, ambiguities, and complexities of academic life. They need to have boundless energy. And most of all, they need to have a sense of humor and in many moments a sense of the absurd.

If presidents have these qualities, they will want to join those of us who, like the president quoted at the beginning of this chapter, want to light candles in thanks for our good fortune at being presidential.

Part II

Becoming an Effective President

8

The Future of the College Presidency

Although, fortunately, a great many talented and committed men and women aspire to become college presidents, there is reason for concern about whether—given the large number of anticipated presidential retirements in the coming years—the pool of capable candidates will be sufficient over time. The 2007 ACE *American College Presidents Study* is explicit about the graying of the presidency, reporting that the average age of college presidents in 2006 was sixty, up from the 1986 average age of fifty-two. Even more instructive numbers are that nearly half of all presidents (49 percent) in 2006 were sixty-one or older compared to 14 percent twenty years earlier. It is a safe assumption that, by 2020, most in this group and even a fair number of their successors will no longer be presidents.

This chapter will explore two different phenomena that are related to the future of the college presidency: the growing lack of interest on the part of chief academic officers (provosts, academic vice presidents, and academic deans) in becoming presidents and the increased interest among boards and search committees for nontraditional and diverse candidates. It will conclude with some suggestions for how higher education as a sector can better prepare future presidents, both traditional and nontraditional.

The Changing Nature of the Presidential Ranks

The 2007 ACE *American College Presidents Study* reports: "Serving as chief academic officer (CAO) has become a more typical route to the presidency. Thirty-one percent of presidents served as provost or CAO prior to becoming president, up from 23 percent in 1986" (p. viii). Many faculty members on search committees have wanted their presidents to have experience as teachers, and in many institutions, as scholars. They have also favored candidates who have practiced shared and transparent governance.

Nevertheless, according to the press release for the 2009 ACE report *The CAO Census: A National Profile of Chief Academic Officers*, even though being a chief academic officer is the most common path to a presidency, only 30 percent of the more than seventeen hundred chief academic officers surveyed intended to seek a presidency, and only 20 percent of them actually became presidents.

In an equally key finding, the 2007 *American College Presidents Study* reports that the average tenure of a chief academic officer is only 4.7 years compared to the significantly longer 8.5-year tenure of all college presidents. Moreover, 21 percent of CAOs leave their position during the first year and 47 percent during their second to fifth years, compared to only 11 percent of presidents who leave during their first year and 27 percent who leave in their second to fifth years. These statistics suggest that even as a great many institutions in the coming years will seek a new president, they may find themselves with a dearth of committed academic deans, vice presidents, and provosts unless they launch new and successful efforts to attract able faculty members to positions of academic leadership.

Colleges and universities suffer a lack of continuity and a sense of instability on campus when key administrators have abbreviated tenures. Some foundations and individual donors may be reluctant to fund institutions where there is a great deal of turnover. Accreditation and rating agencies may have concerns.

Because interest in the presidency seems to be diminishing among chief academic officers, it is not surprising that a greater number of new presidents now come from outside the academy or have been vice presidents in areas other than academic affairs. A report released by the Council of Independent Colleges based on data from a 2008 survey conducted by the American Council of Education notes that 17 percent of new presidents came from outside the academy and 23 percent from such areas as development, student affairs, finance, and enrollment management.

As already noted, boards of trustees and presidential search committees are especially interested in candidates who have facility with budgets, experience in fundraising, and ability to tell the institution's story to alumni, the media, and the higher education sector. They are therefore more willing and sometimes even eager to entertain nontraditional candidates, believing that success in business, government, the diplomatic corps, and nonprofit organizations will translate to the academy and that these nontraditional candidates, as well as college administrators in areas other than academic affairs, will possess skills and experiences that CAOs may not have. Many campuses are also committed to diversity, often defined by ethnicity, gender, and sexual orientation. Search committees, therefore, want to spread the widest net possible.

Hesitation Among Chief Academic Officers

The press release for ACE's 2009 CAO census reports that these academic leaders' main hesitations about becoming presidents are that they "find the nature of presidential work unappealing (66 percent), are ready to retire (32 percent), are concerned about the time demands of the position (27 percent), and don't want to live in a fishbowl (24 percent)." In other words, the same reasons why some CAOs don't want to become president may explain why they are not staying longer in their current position—that is, their work already goes beyond being responsible for the faculty and academic programs and includes at least some of the traditional responsibilities and characteristics of the presidency.

In addition, some chief academic officers are short-timers either because the president who hired them has left the institution and the new president wants to select her or his own chief academic officer or because they find themselves at odds with the president or board. Both of these circumstances may turn capable people away from administration.

Richard Ekman, president of the Council of Independent Colleges, described the situation in his September 19, 2010, piece in the *Chronicle of Higher Education* titled "The Imminent Crisis in College Leadership":

> At both public and independent institutions, academic leaders say presidential duties are inherently unattractive in comparison with their own jobs or those of faculty members. At state colleges, the added discouragement of "sunshine" laws depresses the number of potential candidates, who do not want their candidacies for other positions to be widely known. More than anything else, however, it is the increasingly external orientation of presidential duties that best explains why only 30 percent of all chief academic officers (and just 24 percent of them at independent colleges) still aspire to become college presidents.

A 2010 ad for the dean of the College of Arts and Sciences (CAS) at Lewis & Clark College, which also includes a law school and a graduate school, provides a striking illustration of how decanal responsibilities sometimes include not only the faculty and academic programs but also mirror those of presidents. Specifically, Lewis & Clark (where I served as academic vice president from 1990 to 1992 but in whose search I was not involved) hopes that its new dean will accomplish the following:

- Articulate a vision and plan that will inspire and guide the CAS community

- Develop the financial resources necessary for the college to support its aspirations

- Serve as an effective and progressive manager for faculty and staff

- Promote excellence in teaching and research through enhanced programs and infrastructure

- Create the necessary external partnerships to achieve the vision, within Lewis & Clark and beyond

Even more specifically, the ad further explains that its new dean will:

- Develop a vision for CAS.

- Formulate major institutional goals.

- Distinguish Lewis & Clark from other national liberal arts colleges. Collaborate closely with the president on fundraising.

- Play a leadership role in the next capital campaign.

- Improve how finances are managed at the college.

- Create a new budget system.

Factors Contributing to Short CAO Tenures

There are myriad other reasons why, I believe, chief academic officers choose to be short-timers.

First, most chief academic officers have risen through the faculty ranks only to discover that their new roles require them not only to make judgments about their colleagues in terms of tenure and promotion but often to make difficult budgetary decisions, including perhaps laying off faculty and staff members. Some chief academic officers who have been promoted from within the institution have difficulty saying no to friends and former colleagues. Other chief academic officers want to be loved more than respected and are appalled when they find themselves easily vilified by colleagues who had previously been their close friends.

More than a few chief academic officers have found themselves at odds with their president and even their trustees because they have not been able to think and act institutionally. I know of several provosts who have lost the confidence of their president and in some instances their position because they have been unwilling, in a time of financial shortfalls, to recommend cuts in the academic budget. As a result, their presidents have been reluctant to recommend them as candidates for the presidency because they fear that they will never, as one president (himself a former chief academic officer) put it to me, be able to stop thinking like a faculty member.

Many faculty members are specialists in academic areas, which are more theoretical than applied. When they become chief academic officers, they are suddenly expected to be knowledgeable about and make decisions that affect the very practical areas of admissions, financial aid, and marketing. As at Lewis & Clark, they are often expected to work with the broader community and excel as fundraisers.

Some chief academic officers are unable to go beyond that part of their role that calls for their being advocates for the faculty and the academic programs, finding themselves uncomfortable with the equally important task of advocating for the decisions that the president and the board make, especially when these decisions are unpopular with the faculty.

In addition, there are significant differences in the pace at which faculty members and chief academic officers make decisions, the nature of those decisions, and how they spend their time. Some chief academic officers simply find it difficult to make, often very quickly, the abundance of decisions with which they are confronted on a daily basis because they worry that they either do not have sufficient information or do not have sufficient time to think about it. I know of a superior teacher and scholar who dismayed his faculty colleagues when he became provost because, having been trained to be analytical and think about problems from as many points of view as possible, he was unable to make any decisions—large or small—in a timely way. After six months, members of the search committee who had been his strongest advocates came to the president to tell her they had made a mistake and the faculty was about to take a vote of no confidence in the provost. The president met with the provost, who admitted he was miserable in the job. He resigned and returned to a faculty position. The president did a new search. The next provost, who was decisive, served successfully for nearly a decade.

Finally, some chief academic officers simply miss their old lives. They find themselves chaffing at endless meetings, often chaired by someone else, missing instead the classrooms over which they had presided pretty much as they wished and a schedule over which they had a great deal of control. Many recognize that they prefer contemplation to crisis management.

Interest in Nontraditional Candidates

The 2007 ACE *American College Presidents Study* of long-serving presidents provides evidence of the new emphasis for presidents on external rather than academic affairs. These presidents cited fundraising, accountability and learning assessments, and budget or financial management as the three areas that had increased most in importance during their tenure. Seventy-one percent of presidents of public institutions identified declines in state funding as the reason for the greatest changes in their presidencies, while 74 percent of private college presidents identified increased competition with other colleges as causing the greatest changes. In addition, whereas 57 percent of these presidents noted that when they became president they spent the majority of their time on internal constituencies, they were now spending only 14 percent of their time doing so. A third of them said they were also now spending less time on academic matters.

As committees turn their focus to nontraditional candidates, they usually look for people who have the following:

- A track record of being creative or entrepreneurial

- "The vision thing"

- Experience raising money, perhaps as venture capitalists

- Established connections with an array of successful, often affluent people, whom the committee hopes will become interested in the institution by virtue of those relationships, and who will perhaps join the board or give major gifts

- Experience successfully managing a complex organization

- Responsibility for significant budgets and a track record of making responsible decisions in financial and human resources

- Skill as persuasive and interesting public speakers

- Experience leading strategic planning processes that have led to action, not merely the contemplation of action

- Demonstrated integrity

Many committees also are looking for someone who is charismatic, possessing what they often describe as the "wow" factor, believing that through the force of their personality such individuals will advance the institution.

A comparison of institutional profiles written for presidential searches in 2006 and 2010 for two small private colleges—both of which, I should disclose, I wrote—illustrates the new emphasis on the external rather than internal role of the president.

In 2006, the profile for Ohio Wesleyan University, a nationally ranked liberal arts college, read as follows:

> Ohio Wesleyan faculty, students, staff, alumni, and trustees share a deep commitment to the University, the liberal arts, the art of teaching, the notion that teaching and scholarship enhance one another, academic excellence, and diversity. The community seeks a president who shares those values, embraces the culture of a small liberal arts college, enjoys discourse about ideas, and appreciates (and can provide leadership within) the context of Ohio Wesleyan's tradition of a collegial and participatory approach to planning and governance.
>
> The campus is united in its desire for a president who will engage the campus community in discussions about matters of importance to the institution and who, after careful listening, will make informed decisions. He or she will also clearly communicate to the campus the rationale for such decisions and will work collaboratively with the appropriate constituencies to advance Ohio Wesleyan.
>
> The campus also looks to the next president to turn immediately to reviewing and completing a strategic planning process begun two years ago and also to taking a leadership role in Ohio Wesleyan's next comprehensive fundraising campaign. The campus is eager to cooperate with the president in identifying and recommending to the Board the University's short-term and long-range

strategic priorities and the fundraising goals that derive from those priorities.

What is especially interesting about Ohio Wesleyan's hopes and dreams for its next president at that time is that although the profile indicated the expectation that the next president would be a fundraiser, no preference was given to a proven fundraiser nor was there a call for a president with financial acumen and experience who could allocate and reallocate resources, human and financial, in an equitable way that would enable the university to realize its mission.

The profile for the Elizabethtown College 2010 presidential search has a markedly different emphasis and tone as it describes the challenges it wants its president to meet:

> Elizabethtown's primary challenges are those facing many small private colleges today: the need for more abundant resources because of the College's dependence on tuition and level of debt, the need for funding for the residence halls and fitness center, the need for a larger annual maintenance fund, the desire to be better known beyond the immediate region, and the desire to enroll and retain academically talented students from a broader geographic range. Although for a number of years, the College was able incrementally but steadily to increase its enrollment, improve quality and enjoy strong retention, the economic downturn and changing demographics have brought new challenges: uncertainty about enrollment and the need to increase the financial aid discount for the classes entering in the fall of 2010 and 2011. Given the need for the College to grow the Annual Fund, the endowment (particularly for financial aid), and support for capital/maintenance projects, the new president will need to raise significant funds.

The Quest for Diversity

With few exceptions, presidential search committees identify diversity, broadly defined, as one of their primary goals, and one that they take seriously. Search firms market themselves by documenting their success in recruiting diverse pools of candidates. One firm even advertises itself as "minority- and female-owned."

But despite this focus, the college presidency remains primarily the province of straight white males. As the 2007 ACE *American College Presidents Study* reports, in 2006 the majority of colleges presidents were married white men.

Jacqueline King and Gigi Gomez's ACE 2008 study *On the Pathway to the Presidency: Characteristics of Higher Education's Senior Leadership* reports that the percentage of women presidents rose from 10 percent in 1986 to 23 percent in 2006. This progress has, however, slowed since them. The percentage of women presidents varies significantly by sector. For example, 29 percent of two-year college presidents are women compared with only 13.8 percent of presidents of doctorate-granting institutions. Interestingly, only 63 percent of women presidents are married, compared with 89 percent of their male counterparts.

The study also concludes that the pool of senior administrators who are women is abundant enough to increase the number of women presidents significantly. Specifically, 45 percent of the senior administrators surveyed were women, as were 38 percent of chief academic officers.

The percentage of presidents who are racial or ethnic minorities is much less robust, increasing from 8 percent in 1986 to 14 percent in 2006. Although there are such notable presidents of color as Shirley Jackson at Rensselaer; Ruth Simmons at Brown; Bobby Fong, who after being president of Butler moved in 2011 to Ursinus College; and Frances Cordova at Purdue, among others, when institutions whose mission is to serve people of color are excluded, the number of minority college presidents in 2006 drops to 10 percent.

Moreover, only 16 percent of all senior leaders and fewer than 10 percent of chief academic officers are from ethnic minority groups, a percentage that mirrors the number of faculty members of color.

The concept of diversity in recent years has been expanded to include sexual orientation. For example, several years ago a search committee seeking a provost for one of the top fifty liberal arts colleges in the country was pleased that its list of four finalists included two women and a man of color. Nevertheless, the committee was concerned that the list included no gay candidates. When they learned that one of the two women was a lesbian, they were delighted. In 2008 a flagship state university made national headlines when it named Cornell's provost Biddy Martin, a lesbian, as its chancellor. Grinnell College in 2010 also made headlines when it appointed as its next president Raymond S. Kington, MD, PhD, and MBA, who was a gay black man with a partner and two children. Another example of the increased openness of college campuses is LGBTQ Presidents in Higher Education, a group of gay and lesbian college presidents formed in August 2010. This group is growing in numbers.

It is abundantly clear that higher education, despite the good intentions of many search committees and boards of trustees, has not successfully diversified the presidency so that it, to paraphrase former President Bill Clinton, "looks like America." As I will argue later in this chapter, this lack of success stems in part from the fact that colleges and universities do little if anything to encourage and prepare capable faculty and staff members, whether male or female, whatever their ethnic background, whether gay or straight, to become administrators.

The good news is that most presidents who are women, members of ethnic minority groups, or gay or lesbian find that their presidential role immediately takes precedence over these other aspects of their identity. For example, in a May 29, 2008 piece in *Edge Boston* about the University of Wisconsin's appointment of Biddy Martin,

Ryan Foley quoted Amit Taneja, co-chairman of the Consortium of Higher Education LGBT Resource Professionals, commenting on several openly gay college presidents: "They have been trailblazers in showing to the public that sexual orientation has little to nothing to do with their ability to do their job, although it definitely shapes their worldview just like any other identity."

Nannerl Keohane, former president of Wellesley and Duke, in her 2010 Princeton book *Thinking About Leadership*, offers what I believe to be one of the most insightful statements about presidents. As she puts it, "The demands of institutional leadership outweigh any effects of gender." I am confident that the same is true for ethnicity and sexual orientation. Dr. Keohane writes:

> Even though my leadership of Wellesley or Duke may have had a slightly more inclusive flavor than is typical of [college presidents], I soon learned that the necessities of getting things done, dealing with varied interests, personalities, and perspectives, and making tough decisions and moving on brought me to lead in ways that were generally quite similar to how male leaders of such institutions perform.
>
> If I had been asked after a few years at Wellesley whether women have a distinctive style of leading complex organizations, I would have given a guarded answer, aware of the ways in which women's institutions felt different from those that were traditionally male, but aware also of the demands of organizational governance. After another decade or so, including my time as president of Duke, I had become convinced that the effects of organizational culture and the demands of institutional leadership outweigh any effects of gender.
>
> Today . . . I would agree [with Virginia Woolf and Simone de Beauvoir] that some women (surely not all) in some contexts do lead differently from men; but insofar

as there is a pattern here it stems from socialization and culture expectations, rather than hormones or genes. And like Beauvoir, I cherish the hope that in the future, as more and more women provide leadership, individual women, like men, will simply be regarded as "leaders," not "women leaders," each with our own personal style of dealing with the particular challenges and opportunities leaders face. [pp. 153–154]

Nontraditional Candidates in the Academy

The most appealing college and university vice presidents other than chief academic officers are those who have demonstrated the capacity to be good fundraisers and have successful experience with budgets, admissions, retention, financial aid, institutional positioning, and marketing. Those with such experience have generally been part of institutions where the president and vice presidents together work as a team to deal with all issues of institutional importance. Thus, these vice presidents are well versed in the major issues facing higher education, and unlike candidates from outside the academy, are also comfortable in and knowledgeable about the academic environment.

Advantages for Traditional Candidates

Despite the emphasis on external responsibilities, chief academic officers who have come up through the faculty ranks are often advantaged in a search if their portfolio includes not only academic affairs but other areas that will be germane to their performance as president. Committees are particularly impressed with chief academic officers who, in addition to earning the respect of the faculty and exhibiting genuine interest in students, have demonstrated at least some of the following:

- A record of actual accomplishments in advancing their institution in such areas as curricular reform and the development of new and revenue-producing programs

- Success in leading an institutionwide strategic planning process that benefited the institution

- Success as a fundraiser, at least with foundations but ideally with individual donors as well

- Significant experience with budgets and proven ability to allocate and reallocate human and financial resources

- Ability to make difficult decisions

- Deep understanding of the challenges and opportunities facing American higher education

- Effectiveness as a public speaker and ability to tell the institution's story persuasively

- Experience working with their board of trustees, alumni, and parents.

- A record of fair, inclusive, collaborative, and transparent leadership

The 2009 *National Profile of Chief Academic Officers* suggests that few chief academic officers have experience with external affairs. Specifically, the report notes, "Chief academic officers are modestly engaged in off-campus activities, beyond engaging with other colleges and universities and participating in community relations and outreach. More than 70% said they do little or no fundraising, 75% spend little time on alumni relations, and 64% spend little or no time on government relations."

To expand their portfolio and gain these kinds of experiences, chief academic officers should at least ask their president to allow them to take the lead in cultivating and soliciting potential donors for endowed chairs, academic programs, the library, and academic facilities. If their president wishes, as some do, to be the only person to ask donors for gifts, the president might be willing to include the chief academic officer in the cultivation and solicitation process.

Also, they should make themselves available to their vice president for advancement to help with cultivating donors for academic projects. In coordination with the president and the vice president for advancement, they might visit foundations interested in academic programs and write grant proposals. They can also volunteer to speak to alumni, parents, and community organizations to demonstrate experience in telling an institution's story before audiences large and small.

Finally, they can serve on national professional boards and area nonprofit boards, in order to be able to make the case that they are already involved in activities that benefit the institution's reputation and to gain more experience in financial and governance affairs.

Recommendations for Nontraditional Candidates

Just as chief academic officers benefit from broader experiences outside the academic arena, so nontraditional candidates need to be versed in the academic enterprise. For example, they need to understand at least the following:

- The intricacies of shared governance

- The hiring, tenure, and promotion processes in the academy

- Curricular reform and the politics accompanying curricular changes

- Enrollment practices, opportunities, and challenges such as the changing demographics in a number of geographic areas

- Financial aid discounting

- The importance of net tuition revenue

- The ways in which academic and student affairs are increasingly being integrated

- Interdisciplinary programs

- The "amenities wars"

- The role of athletics and the nature of the various NCAA divisions, and if pertinent, the nature of NAIA

- The crisis of excessive drinking on college campuses

- The place of fraternities and sororities on campuses

- The role and cost of instructional technology

Nontraditional candidates would benefit from regularly reading *Inside Higher Ed*, the *Chronicle of Higher Education*, the *Chronicle of Philanthropy*, and *Trusteeship*. They might meet with several presidents at institutions comparable to the one whose presidency they seek. They should ask questions of the search consultant where they are candidates, and also ask them for a bit of coaching.

Even when they have great potential, if they do not have that kind of knowledge they may well harm their candidacies because they will make mistakes out of naiveté. Often these mistakes unwittingly violate some protocol indigenous to higher education. A few examples will make the point:

- A successful corporate CEO destroyed her candidacy by beginning her interview with the search committee by laying out the detailed blueprint for action she would take if she were to become president. She had yet to set foot on the campus and had had no conversations about the institution's mission and goals with any member of the campus community or the board. She thought she was being appropriately visionary and proactive, exhibiting those qualities that had led her to her current success. The committee thought she was being presumptuous. They also faulted her for being disinterested in the history, culture, and values of the college.

- Several candidates, reading in the institutional profile that one of their roles would be to raise the reputation of the institution, described how well connected they were in political and cultural circles. They had erroneously assumed that telling the committee about the breadth of their connections would suggest their ability to bring the institution national visibility and significant gifts. The committee saw each of them as name-droppers.

- A corporate CEO alienated the search committee at a college committed to undergraduate liberal arts education when he began his interview by asserting that the college needed, if it were to survive, to add a series of online preprofessional graduate programs. Because this proposal ran counter to the institution's mission, the search committee rejected him out of hand.

- A candidate who was highly placed in a major corporation angered several trustee members of the search committee by vehemently criticizing the university's choice of peer and aspirant institutions, a group that the board had spent a great deal of time reviewing and approving. He mistakenly thought he was showing the committee that he had done his homework and understood the university's competitive position.

- The president of an admired nonprofit gave the committee pause by declaring that he planned to teach every semester, have regular sleepovers in the residence halls, and would attend virtually all campus events. By focusing on an on-campus role, he unwittingly negated the very reason why the committee was interested in him: his perceived ability to raise funds, connect with alumni and donors, and speak nationally on behalf of the institution.

But for candidates who are unfamiliar with the norms of the academy, coaching can and does work. One corporate leader mightily impressed the search committee at his semifinalist interview but nevertheless worried some of them because he talked about faculty positions not as "lines" but as "boxes." Because they were otherwise so impressed, the committee invited him for a campus visit and asked me to counsel him not to use corporate language during that visit. He took that advice and was offered the position.

To mitigate the potential dissonance between nontraditional candidates and search committees, I encourage committees to focus on candidates who at some point in their lives have had experience in an institution like theirs, either as a student, a faculty member, an administrator, or a trustee. I cite examples of successful nontraditional candidates who were graduates of the institutions that appointed them. I note that other successful nontraditional candidates have served as trustees, often chairing the academic affairs, finance, or development committees of the board and thereby gaining an understanding of the contemporary higher education landscape. Some candidates who were trustees also differentiated themselves because they had, as trustees, partnered with the vice president for advancement and the president in fundraising.

Leadership Programs

There are a few leadership development opportunities for aspiring presidents, but most of these programs are small in size and last from only a few days to a few weeks, thereby limiting the number of people who can take advantage of them. The programs include the Council of Independent Colleges (CIC) annual Chief Academic Officers Institute; the American Council of Education (ACE) fellowships and its Institute for Chief Academic Officers; the American Association of State Colleges and Universities' (AASCU) Millennium Leadership Initiative (MLI); the two-week Harvard Institute for Educational Management (IEM); the Higher

Education Resource Services Institutes (HERS) Advancing Women Leaders in Higher Education Administration program; and the new American Academic Leadership Institute (AALI) program titled Academic Leadership for the 21st Century: A Program for Provosts and Chief Academic Officers to Prepare for the Presidency, which is sponsored by CIC and AASCU and funded by Academic Search, Inc. Several of these programs have an ongoing component in which sitting presidents mentor those aspiring to become presidents. There are no comparable programs for nontraditional candidates.

The excellent five-day Harvard Seminar for New Presidents is available annually to approximately forty-five new presidents from both traditional and nontraditional backgrounds.

Attracting Good People

The higher education sector needs to be intentional about and proactive in attracting capable people, whether traditional or non-traditional, to academic administration at the senior levels and especially the presidency. On some level, each group—traditional and nontraditional candidates—will need to have the knowledge, understanding, and skills of the other group.

Faculty Members

Despite the need for strong academic leadership, with few exceptions colleges and universities do almost no succession planning and provide little training for future leaders. To interest talented faulty members in administration, these institutions, the higher educational associations, and I would argue, the professional disciplinary organizations, need to encourage those who exhibit leadership potential to prepare to become department chairs, program directors, and associate deans and then eventually deans, provosts, or chief academic officers, and perhaps presidents. Certainly, faculty members understand the importance of having a chief academic officer who bears primary responsibility for the health, quality, and integrity of the academic programs, the faculty, the curriculum, the library, and often such areas as athletics and technology. They also need to understand the great satisfaction that comes from doing this work well and see themselves playing this important role.

There are a few exceptions. Some large research universities are beginning to set up such programs for department chairs, and at least one community college in the West has done the same. The American Council on Education offers an institute for department chairs and provides an online resource guide of reading materials for that group. But in most instances, neither department chairs nor faculty members who assume leadership positions as members of a faculty senate are provided with any formal orientation. Deans and academic vice presidents similarly usually learn by doing.

Many faculty members have a negative view of administration, a view that institutional practices often reinforce. For instance, on many campuses, faculty members rotate in and out of the position of department chair, thinking of it as an onerous duty, something akin to extended jury duty. They also understand that their tenure will be a brief one and that the position will in a few years rotate to someone else, who will be reviewing them and scheduling their classes. Because they see this administrative role as a responsibility that takes them away from their normal lives, it is not surprising that even some faculty members who are seeking to move into administration tell search committees that they are "going over to the dark side." (The phrase tends to lead committees to look unfavorably on these candidates for appearing ambivalent about becoming administrators.)

I'd like to make several recommendations about initiatives that colleges and universities can and should undertake to pre-pare promising faculty members to be effective administrators with the goal of eventually moving into the upper levels of adminis-tration. For example, chief academic officers need intentionally to provide department chairs with the knowledge that they need to do their jobs well. Chief academic officers might, with other senior staff members, offer a formal orientation program for new department chairs with the goal of ensuring that they understand the following:

- The importance of thinking institutionally, not just departmentally.

- The institution's mission and its strategic priorities.

- The budgeting process (including the major budget drivers) and the role department chairs today play in the budgeting process. Whereas a decade ago, chairs were usually given an opportunity to request additions to their departmental operating budgets, their main budget responsibility was to oversee budgets handed to them from above to ensure that the department followed institutional guidelines and did not spend more than allocated. Today chairs often need to make cuts rather than ask for new resources and do so in the context of institutional rather than departmental needs and priorities.

- The current state of admissions and retention, including information about how chairs and their faculty colleagues can assist in these two critical areas.

- Ways that the institution seeks to integrate the curriculum and co-curricular programs.

- How the student affairs staff can collaborate with and provide support to department chairs and other members of the faculty as well as students.

- Fundraising goals, particularly relating to the academic programs.

Staff Members

Staff member training more often than not is focused on developing the skills these individuals need for their current position. It seldom focuses on preparing people to move up the administrative hierarchy. Although, as noted earlier, greater numbers of vice presidents are promoted from within than are presidents, it is often the case that those who wish to be promoted to senior positions need to move to a new institution to do so. Unfortunately, at that new institution, they need to learn their new role while on the job.

Candidates from Outside the Academy

Regardless of their backgrounds, as already noted, there are to my knowledge no programs whose purpose is to prepare people from outside the academy for presidencies. There is a crying need for such programs, because no matter how talented an administrator may be in the corporate sector, the military, the diplomatic corps, Congress, the government, or foundations, making things happen on college campuses is a very different matter. The emphasis on process, often at the expense of outcome, will be foreign and often frustrating to someone who is used to making judgments in terms of cost or benefit to the bottom line and who is used to making unilateral decisions.

The Mixed News about Candidate Pools

The good news is that many more people aspire to become college presidents than are actually offered the position. Every applicant pool with which I have worked has included at least eight to twelve people—sometimes, happily, more—who in the search committee's judgment on paper at least met most or all of the assessment criteria and interested the committee enough that it wanted to interview them. Yet often when very capable people like these are interviewed, they fail to make the case that they are well prepared and suited for a presidency.

Most of these candidates do have talent and promise. If colleges, universities, and higher education associations wish to take advantage of that talent and realize that promise, they are going to have to be much more intentional than they are now in attracting and preparing a new cadre of effective leaders. The next chapter turns to this final subject.

9

Back to the Beginning: The Search Process

This, the final chapter of the book, will return to the beginning, focusing on the presidential search process.

Being a candidate for a presidency is hard work. It is time-consuming and often emotionally taxing. Yet, those candidates who see their candidacy as an opportunity to understand a college or university's story and to tell their own story in a way that attracts the institution often advance to the level of semifinalist and above. Even if they ultimately are not offered the job, almost all of them tell me how much they learned through the process about higher education, about the institution in question, and most of all about themselves. In the best of all worlds, they and the college have been enriched by their encounter.

In every search there are a number of candidates who, although not selected for what commonly are referred to as "neutral site" or "airport" interviews—that is, an initial in-person interview—nevertheless have much to offer. Generally, they do not become semifinalists because they are not as seasoned as other candidates; they have had no experience in institutions like the one to which they are applying and did not make the case that their experience was transferable; they did not address or fulfill the criteria outlined in the ad and profile; they have only been in their current position a short time and did not explain why they wished to leave that position; they have a history of changing positions every few years, and again, offered no explanation why; or they submitted letters that contained typographical, spelling, or grammatical errors.

The Importance of "Fit"

Candidates are inevitably confronted with variables they cannot control, most notably the strength of their competition and the chemistry between them, the search committee, and if they advance to the finalist stage, the campus generally. Because every campus has its own culture, its own traditions, even its own idiosyncrasies, the notion of fit is real. Although some committees may, even unconsciously, use the idea of fit to justify decisions based on bias rather than substance, my own experience has been that most committees are genuinely committed to fairness.

Moreover, every committee with which I have worked has believed that every candidate they decided to interview had the experience and abilities to be an effective president. What they hope to discover in their interview is which ones share their values, understand and honor their culture, and appear to be people with whom they could happily interact. On many levels, this is the most subjective and even intuitive part of the process.

Being told after an interview that the committee has selected a finalist or finalists with whom they think the fit is better is especially hard for those who, no matter how talented, cannot change this piece of the puzzle. Yet candidates need to recognize that while the fit was not right at this particular institution, it may be absolutely right at another institution. For example, I have seen candidates who were not advanced to the finalist stage at one institution but, a year later, after a comparable interview with a different institution, were enthusiastically chosen as its president.

Several examples will illustrate the point.

- In a search that had attracted more than one hundred candidates, the committee believed that at least twenty-five had the experience and ability to be successful presidents. After much discussion, the committee decided to interview eleven semifinalists. Based on those interviews, they selected two for campus visits. The first was a very talented, charismatic executive vice president whose airport interview led several committee members to tell me they were thrilled that they had just met their next president. The second was very different in experience and temperament. A prize-winning teacher and a nationally known scholar, he had as a provost developed exciting new programs and raised a good deal of money. Both did well on their campus visits but the second candidate— because of his more extensive experience and demonstrated success—became the unanimous choice of the committee and the board. The first candidate would have prevailed if his competitor had not been in the search.

- Two finalists for a presidency at a private liberal arts college presented comparable views about the role of athletics in that setting. The campus reacted negatively to the first finalist and embraced his competitor. The difference was not in the substance of what each person said but in the style in which they discussed this and other issues. The first candidate was brutally honest. The second was as candid but came across as empathetic and reassuring. The campus wanted empathy and reassurance.

- A campus responded positively to what they judged to be the independent spirit and confidence of a candidate they chose as president, whereas a year earlier, a different and less prestigious campus had interpreted that independence and confidence as arrogance.

- A candidate with an abundance of the "vision thing" excited one
  campus with her ideas, but seemed presumptuous to a different
  campus.

When candidates have an unhappy campus visit, I tell them that they were fortunate to learn that the match wasn't right before taking their vows, because if something seemed a problem at the courtship stage it almost certainly would have become a significant source of tension once the relationship had been consummated.

Challenges Facing Internal Candidates

The decision to hire a search consultant to facilitate a national presidential search in and of itself suggests the institution's interest in or at least openness to selecting a president from outside its own ranks. In fact, according to the 2007 ACE *American College President Study*, more than half of presidential searches today are facilitated by search consultants, compared with only 12 percent before 1984.

According to the 2008 survey of campus human resources professionals conducted by ACE in conjunction with the College and University Professional Association for Human Resources (CUPA-HR) titled *On the Pathway to the Presidency: Characteristics of Higher Education's Senior Leadership*, although 49 percent of senior administrators were internal candidates for their position, only 27.6 percent of presidents were promoted from within. The number of successful internal candidates in liberal arts colleges and comprehensive universities is even smaller: 21.3 percent and 22.5 percent, respectively.

So why are colleges and universities inclined to hire from outside?

- Boards of trustees are interested in hiring the very best person in the nation and so are reluctant to limit their pool to candidates from within their institution.

- The interest in diversity leads boards to want the largest possible pool from which to choose their next president.

- Institutions seeking change tend to believe that candidates with experience at other institutions will bring in new ideas; in contrast, they fear that internal candidates may not be able to go beyond the status quo.

- Internal candidates who have held senior administrative positions will inevitably have made decisions that not everyone supports.

- Because many faculty members disdain administrative work, their talented colleagues may be discouraged from moving into the role of department chair, dean, or academic vice president or provost.

Internal candidates often create complexity for presidential search committees, particularly if they have been named interim president or hold a vice presidency. For this reason, when I am consulted about the choice of interim president, I encourage institutions to name someone who explicitly will not be a candidate for the presidency.

Search committees genuinely wish to treat every candidate equally, but they inevitably bring to the table greater knowledge about internal candidates than about most external candidates. Moreover, although most external candidates do not wish their candidacies to be known unless they are among the finalists, many internal candidates have shared their interest in the position, leading some of their friends and colleagues to lobby search committee members. Many committees worry that if they do not choose a respected colleague to be their next president, she or he might leave the institution. Finally, committees become concerned the presence of an internal candidate might discourage some external candidates from applying. They are right in that often the first question potential candidates ask is whether there is an internal candidate, and if so, whether the search is an authentic one.

In light of these complexities and after discussions with the search committee, I frequently advise people on campus who wish to be candidates not to put themselves forward formally but rather to let me privately and confidentially tell the committee about their interest. Because these candidates' abilities are well known to at least the campus members of the committee, and because searches usually remain open until an appointment is made, committees always have the option—after reviewing the materials from external candidates—to let me know if they want me to encourage their interested colleague to become a formal candidate. Those who choose not to put themselves forward simply tell the people who have been encouraging them that they have decided not to do so at this point because they believe it to be in the best interests of the institution to conduct a national search uncompromised by their presence.

In one such case, the committee did, after reviewing the external candidates, decide it wished the person in the interim position to become a formal candidate. The person did so confidentially, was formally interviewed as a semifinalist, was brought for a successful campus visit as a finalist, and was appointed to the position. In a very different and less happy case, an interim president quite publicly and immediately announced in her blog to the campus and alumni that she was applying for the permanent position. She then persuaded the vice presidents that if someone came in from outside, their vice presidential positions would almost certainly be in jeopardy, but that she would guarantee them ongoing employment. Although the vice presidents all became her advocates, the tactic back-fired when it became known to the search committee, which was offended by it. The presidency went to an external candidate.

Those potential internal candidates who have decided not to apply formally at the beginning of a search later told me that they were glad they had made that choice. In most instances, once they met the person the committee had selected, they realized they would not have successfully competed against him or her. They were glad that they did not suffer the public embarrassment of having been passed over. They were also glad that they were able to establish a positive working relationship with their new president, uncomplicated by the sense that they had been competitors.

How Candidates Can Influence Searches

The "fit" factor aside, candidates are able to influence many aspects of the search. Specifically, they can at the outset engage the committee by crafting a compelling cover letter, creating a complete and interesting curriculum vitae (CV), and selecting their references strategically. The failure to do any one of these things is likely to torpedo their candidacy.

Well-Written Cover Letters

The best-received candidates submit well-written, interesting, and often inspiring letters of interest. Successful letters answer the questions: Why this institution? Why me? Why now? Such letters also demonstrate that the candidates have done their homework, understand the institution's strengths, challenges, and opportunities and are very interested in the position. These letters explicitly make the case that the writers possess the experience, accomplishments, and credentials that the position requires, giving the committee confidence that they have been effective in fulfilling many of the responsibilities that will be critical to a successful presidency.

Such letters also explicitly demonstrate what it is in the candidates' background that would appeal to the search committee. For instance, as the previous chapter suggests, if the college has made it clear that it wants its next president to be a successful fundraiser, even if candidates have never solicited individual gifts, they should highlight any relevant experience, including any fundraising done as members of nonprofit boards or at previous institutions.

Candidates serve themselves well by addressing clearly and crisply in the first few paragraphs of their cover letter any issues that they anticipate might be of concern to the committee. For example, if they have only been in their current job for two or three years, committees will want to know why they are considering a move. If their experience has been only in private institutions and they are applying for a job at a public university (or vice versa), they should explain why they believe they could successfully make that transition and think doing so would be desirable not just for them but for the institution. If they have gaps in their CV they should briefly explain the reasons why. Committees today understand breaks from professional pursuits, for example, for child rearing or caring for an ailing relative.

Writing an excellent letter takes care and time. It demands that candidates learn all that they can about the college or university by reading and thinking not only about the ad and the institutional profile but also about pertinent materials on the college's website.

The least compelling letters (other than those that are poorly written) speak only about the candidates' experience with no reference at all to the hiring institution or the criteria that the search committee has developed. Some of these letters come from perennial applicants who have developed a template for letters of application. These stock letters usually arrive within a day or two of the ad's appearance.

Committees generally dismiss these "generic" or "to whom it may concern" letters, recognizing that they are all-purpose letters that candidates have prepared to send in response to every ad that strikes their fancy (and even to some that do not). These letters tend to follow the same pattern. They begin with a paragraph that mentions the hiring institution's name, but the body of the letter focuses exclusively on the candidates' self-perceived strengths and accomplishments without regard to the institution in question. They usually end with a reiteration of how much the candidates want the position.

This approach has its dangers. One candidate submitted her template by mistake. Her letter of application therefore began with a statement that said something like, "Dear [name of chair of search committee], This is to apply for [name of position] at [name of school]. I am sure that I would be a great [name of position] at [name of school]. Indeed, I have spent my life preparing to be [name of position] at [name of school]." This application provided the committee with some welcome comic relief, but its members had no interest in the candidate. Other candidates apparently forgot to use the "replace" function on their computers when they send variations of the same letter to multiple institutions. As a result, their letters first express interest in the institution in question only to later describe the candidate's hope to become president of an altogether different but competitor college that is also looking for a president. In all such instances, committees eliminate these candidates, deciding that they want a president who is attentive to detail.

A Tailored CV

In contrast to candidates for a faculty position, presidential candidates do not need to provide a list of every book and essay they have published, every paper they have presented, and every conference they have attended, although they might list a sampling of important ones under such headings as "Selected Publications," "Selected Presentations," and "Selected Conferences." They should also understand that most trustees on search committees are accustomed to résumés of a page or two and will out of hand reject those candidates whose CV's are excessively long. The candidate who submitted a fifty-eight page résumé occasioned a good deal of comment, but committee members rejected him for having poor judgment, with most admitting that they stopped reading after page five.

In my experience, committees do want to see dates on CV's, and so when candidates omit the dates of their degrees or the positions they've held, committee members become distracted trying to figure them out. The assumption is generally that the candidates do not want to reveal their age, but the omission of dates attracts more attention than the dates would. (Candidates today should be reassured that committees now do often think of sixty as the new forty, as the saying goes.)

Effective CV's very quickly tell their readers the most salient facts about the candidates: when and where they received their degrees and in what areas, the positions they've held (beginning with their current job and working backward), and any important professional accomplishments. At the same time, the CV should not simply restate the information provided in the cover letter.

Committees tend to think poorly of candidates who use the term ABD in their CV as if having "all but the dissertation" is akin to earning a degree. In this case, more information is better. For example, the CV might include a category for "Graduate Work" that notes whether the required coursework and exams have been completed, the status of the Ph.D. dissertation, and its expected completion date, if there is one.

Committees also are skeptical of candidates who list such experiences as participating in the Harvard Institute for Educational Management under the category of "Education." Most would see such an activity as professional development.

Good References

When an ad calls for references to be included with the application materials, candidates should again think carefully about those they ask to speak for them. Ideally, the list will include a faculty member, several senior administrators, and at least one trustee with whom the candidate has worked.

Some candidates seem to believe that if their CV includes the names of extremely prominent people, committees will be impressed. They are right, assuming that those prominent people can actually speak knowledgeably about the candidates. One candidate who provided a list with nearly twice as many names as the ad requested, most of them major public figures, interested the committee a great deal. The problem: when committee members called these references, they learned that the candidate had not let them know that they would be called. Even more significantly, most of them didn't remember the candidate. The committee thus learned much from these references—not only about the quality of the candidate's work but also about his integrity and his judgment.

Whether the references are prominent or not, it makes sense for candidates to ask people for permission to list them. It also makes sense for them to provide the reference with a brief description of the job being sought and some insight into why the position attracts them.

Although committees can rightly assume that most of those listed as references at this stage of the process will be favorable to the candidate, they nevertheless often learn a great deal from these conversations. For example, most references will be forthcoming about whether candidates are ready to be or are capable of becoming presidents.

Information from Search Consultants

If the search is facilitated by a consultant, it is always wise for candidates, after they have read the ad and institutional profile and reviewed the institution's website, to ask the consultant for a conversation that might expand on the issues described in the ad and profile. Prior to the conversation, candidates should make a list of the questions they wish to ask. For example, asking a consultant, "Tell me what this college is looking for in a president" or asking questions already answered in the profile are not likely to impress the consultant. Questions that probe more deeply into the information the candidate already has received will suggest that the candidate is both serious and informed. Well-informed candidates also impress search committees. It is instructive that all of the successful presidential candidates with whom I've worked in my capacity as a consultant have asked extremely insightful and thoughtful questions, not only at the outset of the search but as it progressed.

The Interview

The first interview is the "neutral site" interview. Most search committees narrow their applicant pool to those they wish to interview at an off-campus site. Usually, committees will interview eight to ten semifinalists, although some committees interview more and some less. The number depends in part on the quality of the pool. These interviews range from one to two hours in general. Normally, the entire committee interviews each candidate, although some committees divide themselves in half, with each group interviewing each candidate for an hour. Occasionally, a committee will give candidates questions in advance of the interview.

Preparing for the Interview

Successful candidates demonstrate an understanding of the institution's mission, strategic plan, financial circumstance including its level of debt and its capacity for future borrowing, fundraising results, and percent of alumni who give to their alma mater. They will have thought about patterns of first-year and transfer admissions, retention, graduation rates, and the financial aid discount. They will be well versed in the institution's curriculum, service learning, the role of athletics, the quality of the facilities, and the level of deferred maintenance. They will have read any institutional histories. For example, one candidate earned the committee's endorsement when he was questioned about what he was currently reading and was able to answer by naming a history of the college.

As already mentioned, candidates who can't find answers to factual questions in the profile or on the institution's website should feel free, before their interview, to turn to the search consultant, or if the institution is doing the search on its own, the committee's executive secretary. Usually, the institution will be glad to share information with candidates at this stage of the search.

So what is it that creates the impression that some talented and experienced candidates are presidential and others are not?

The Successful Interview

In my experience, successful candidates answer most questions directly and concisely, perhaps illustrating their answer with only one pertinent example from their own experience.

They come to interviews expecting not only to be asked questions but also to have formulated their own probing questions. Thus, they do not ask factual questions but rather ask committee members to interpret what they have learned. Interviewing for a presidency on a campus where retention had been identified as a major problem, the strongest candidate did not ask, "What are your retention numbers?" but rather, "Do you have reliable data on why 25 percent of your first-semester freshmen leave, what actions have you taken to improve retention, and what have you learned along the way?"

They immediately, and in an understated way, transform the interview from a question-and-answer session into a genuine and often lively conversation. They do so because in addition to listening carefully to and answering questions, they again ask insightful questions of their own. For example, one successful candidate asked committee members to envision that it was a decade later and the college had met its most important goals. How, she then asked, would the institution look, what would the differences be from its current profile, and why had the college been so successful? Committee members found the question so interesting that, had the chair allowed it, they would have taken up the entire interview time sharing their views. With this question, the candidate engaged the committee. She also learned through their answers a good deal that helped her shape her response to later questions.

Successful candidates readily admit when they don't know an answer, although if this happens too often, they will disqualify themselves for not having done their homework.

When asked open-ended and often loaded questions such as "What is your position on fraternities and sororities?" and "What do you think about athletics?" they ask for context. Then, after understanding a bit more about what is behind the question, they articulate a set of values that would govern their actions as president rather than presuming—without knowing the institution better—to outline a specific course of action.

They have taken the time to learn something about the search committee members. Although many colleges post short bios of these individuals on their search web page, most committees are impressed by candidates who have googled them (although one search committee member was unhappy that she had been googled, saying that it made her feel stalked). In contrast, the candidate who asked the student representative how the volleyball team was doing won lots of points for knowing that the student played volleyball. The faculty members and trustees on the committee were even more pleased that the candidate was paying attention to the student. Another candidate, when introduced to a committee member who was both a trustee and the parent of a recent graduate, asked why the trustee's daughter had chosen the college, what the quality of her experience had been, and what she was doing now. He too made allies even before the questioning had begun.

Successful candidates show that they have a sense humor. This is not to suggest that they tell jokes. Quite the contrary. But they do need to smile and make others in the room smile. When committees and the candidate share some laughter, that is usually a sign of the chemistry being right.

College presidents need to play handball, and so do candidates. That is, candidates need to be at ease responding to questions that seem to come out of nowhere. One candidate, for example, graciously fielded an illegal and inappropriate question from a trustee about his religion. Other committee members were upset by the question and grateful to the candidate for being gracious. He was invited for a campus interview, but based in part on his concern that this question suggested that his religious background might be a concern to some campus constituencies, declined the invitation.

Interview Problems

Being selected for an interview and interviewing successfully are two different matters. Candidates who on paper were especially attractive to the committee and whose references were sparkling have doomed their candidacy because they have spoken in a monotone or so quietly the committee had difficulty hearing them, failed to make eye contact with the committee, used crass language, failed to answer the questions asked of them, were critical of current or former colleagues, violated confidentiality, or were pedantic.

Failing to Answer Questions Effectively

Far too many talented candidates harm their candidacy by failing to answer the committee's questions. Sometimes they are so eager to demonstrate what they know that they provide answers to the questions they wish they had been asked rather than the ones that they were asked. That may work for media sound bites, but committee members—who have thought long and hard about their questions—are not happy with what one called "a diversionary tactic." Other candidates seem to hear the questions selectively, focusing on an element in a question rather than the question itself. For example, a candidate asked about how he would balance his on-campus and external responsibilities, such as attending athletic events versus fundraising, replied with an in-depth discussion of the role of athletics on a college campus. Another candidate, asked how she would deal with a campus crisis, got lost in a story about problems with fraternities and sororities. Because the campus for which she was interviewing did not have a Greek system, the committee was baffled by her response.

Other candidates lose support by being longwinded. Although some of this may be caused by nervousness, committees imagine candidates in all the settings where presidents speak. These verbose candidates harm their candidacies in two ways. First, their listeners become restless. Indeed, a candidate who "overtalked" her answers led the board chair to observe privately, "I don't think I could tolerate board meetings listening to that voice go on and on." Second, by talking too much, candidates often prevent the committee from asking questions they deem important and discourage them from asking follow-up questions.

Being Critical

A surprising number of candidates drop out of contention because they are negative about others. In one memorable interview, a candidate railed against how she had been discriminated against by her president, citing a long and angry tale of woe, including her failed lawsuit against him. Her anger worried the committee. Coincidentally and ironically, that president was also a candidate. His references had already told committee members about how calm and fair he was, describing an instance when he had been falsely accused of discrimination. Another candidate lost favor with the committee when he complained about his treatment at the hand of his last two presidents. Then there was the candidate who criticized his current board chair. In all instances, committee members did not advance these candidates, imagining that over time these candidates would turn on them.

One such negative candidate spent a good deal of the interview talking about all the problems facing his current institution without once praising it or offering possible solutions to the problems he described.

Violating Confidentiality

Some candidates also make the fatal mistake of violating the confidentiality of matters on their own campus. One such candidate, a provost, described how he had fired a dean. Another, asked to describe a contentious situation, described a lawsuit about a tenure decision. A third described an unhappy personnel decision with an employee with a substance abuse problem. In each instance, the stories contained enough specificity that the committee members could, had they wanted to, have identified the people being described. Although each of these candidates had strengths, those strengths became irrelevant to the committees that valued confidentiality about personnel matters.

Being "Too Academic"

Both trustees and faculty members have eliminated candidates who seemed to them to be "too academic" or "too intellectual." At first, those comments baffled me, but after probing I learned that what some of these committees meant was that the candidates appeared to be pedantic and more interested in what they perceived to be teaching than learning or listening. A very capable provost during his on-campus visit at the forum for the faculty gave such detailed answers about the curriculum at his home institution that he had time to answer only two questions whereas his competitors had each fielded at least a dozen during the same amount of time. Other committees deeply admired some chief academic officers but worried that they did not demonstrate an ability to move from working with the faculty to thinking institutionally. That perception came from the fact that in answering questions, these candidates only discussed faculty matters.

Communicating Ambivalence

Some candidates exhibit ambivalence either about the position or the institution. One committee rejected a candidate who, they concluded, seemed to want the committee to provide her with career counseling. Another candidate spent part of his interview criticizing the college interviewing him. He explained with unbecoming arrogance that he thought the committee would benefit from his critique. An especially strong candidate refused the offer of the committee chair to arrange a campus visit for him even though he had time between his interview and his flight out to do so. Although he was in fact very interested in the position, his refusal to take the campus tour gave the opposite message, and the committee decided not to make him a finalist. Another also very promising candidate alienated members of the search committee when she told them that she had asked someone to drive her the several hours from her home to the interview so that she could read the materials the college had sent her during the drive. Although it turned out that this candidate had previously done her homework, the committee assumed that she had not.

Clearly, candidates should be sure before they accept an invitation to an interview that, barring the unforeseen, they are genuinely interested in the position. This doesn't mean that by agreeing to an interview, they are agreeing to take the job, but it does mean that they have come to terms with such critical questions as these: Would my spouse or partner be willing to move to this new location? Does the location work for me? Am I sure that I want to do the work that the position will require?

Sadly, I have seen candidates who would otherwise have been invited for campus visits disqualify themselves because they said things like the following:

- I haven't talked to my husband about this move, and I'm not sure whether he will be OK with it.

- I think that moving may prove to be too much of a problem for our teenage son but if I'm offered the job, my wife and I will think long and hard about it.

- I do have a concern about moving to the Midwest since I can't imagine living anywhere but on one of the coasts.

- I'm not sure that I want to be a president, but I thought that this interview might help me make up my mind.

• I probably wouldn't have come for this interview, but the search consultant was so persuasive that here I am.

Appearance Does Matter

It is absolutely the case that appearance matters, and unfortunately it seems to matter more when the candidate is a woman (as Chapter Two suggests, this concern with appearance persists for women who become presidents). Simply stated, at first (and even at second and third) glance, men have fewer problems than women do in looking presidential. Men can wear a dark suit, an ironed shirt, and a presentable tie. Women have many more decisions to make. Should they wear a suit, a dress, or—now that Hillary Clinton has changed expectations in this regard—a pantsuit? If a skirt or a dress, how long? Neutral hose or tights? How high a heel? What about hairstyle?

The following stories about candidates whose appearance was a negative are drawn not merely from my experience but from that of friends and colleagues.

• A very capable candidate alienated the search committee because of her abundant makeup.

• An otherwise stylish candidate who had hairsprayed "big hair" that didn't move as she nodded her head distracted committee members from her answers because of their fascination with this hair that seemed to have its own separate life.

• At the other end of the spectrum, a candidate who wore no makeup at all was viewed negatively because she appeared "unfinished" and "washed out."

• Another candidate lost votes because her heavy dark hiking shoes and her ill-fitting dress made her appear "frumpish."

- A very attractive candidate showed up for her interview in a jogging suit, suggesting to the committee that the interview was unimportant to her.

There are, of course, men whose appearance serves to distance committees: a bold tie that by the committee's standards is ugly, an extravagant mustache that a committee finds off-putting, clothes that don't fit and colors that clash. But more often than not, such fashion problems tend to be ignored in men.

Some Caveats

Candidates often falter because they fail to acknowledge the executive secretary to the search committee. In one instance, a semifinalist walked around the room to introduce himself to committee members but ignored the executive secretary with whom he had had frequent contact. The next ninety minutes were pro forma. The committee had already concluded that this was a person who would not respect the staff.

Candidates who rely on rhetorical fillers like "um" and "you know" also don't impress committees. One search committee member saw it as his role to keep track of such infelicities and kept a running tally of how often each candidate uttered such phrases.

Candidates who only focus on the wonders of their home institution and altogether ignore the hiring institution in their remarks make committees wonder why they want to make a move.

Candidates who give the sense that they want the job because they believe that it will be less challenging than their current job also disqualify themselves. A president of a large public institution, for example, made the fatal mistake of telling the committee for a small private liberal arts college that he was tired of working so hard and looked forward to being on a smaller campus with a less demanding pace. Another candidate explained that he was interested in the position for which he was interviewing because the institution was in relatively good financial shape and so would be easier to manage.

Mystical Moments

Some candidates rise to the top of the committee's list because of their personal charm and their especially insightful answers. In such instances, something almost mystical happens during the interview. Indeed, I have been struck by how quickly and easily almost every presidential search committee with which I have worked has agreed on which interview candidates they envision as their next president. In the debriefing sessions after these interviews, I consistently hear committee members say that they "knew" almost immediately that particular candidates would be a superb choice.

When committee members in an interview begin to think favorably about a candidate, there is a palpable shift in both the tone and the texture of the interview. Specifically, even as the committee continues to ask questions, at least some members begin to court the candidate. Committee members begin to go "off-script" and ask questions that are not on the agreed-upon list but are important to them. They do so because they have begun to care about what this candidate thinks. In such interviews, as noted earlier, there also tends to be a fair amount of laughter.

There is an equally discernible shift when a promising candidate is disappointing in person. In such instances, the committee generally becomes less animated. Some people begin to doodle. Others glance at their watches. Occasionally, someone sneaks a look at his or her Blackberry or iPhone. Perceptive candidates recognize this phenomenon and find a way to engage the committee going forward. Other candidates, to their disadvantage, either do not read the "body language" of the committee or simply don't know how to gain the committee's attention.

Candidates should be reassured that committee members do want to give every candidate full and fair consideration, and so they do spend most of the interview and the group's ensuing deliberations seeking to affirm or deny their initial impressions, whether positive or negative. After the interviews, they listen hard to the judgments of their committee colleagues and are often persuaded by them. But if their initial impression is a shared one, it will generally prevail.

The Campus Visit

If candidates are invited, generally with spouses or partners and sometimes with children who are still living at home, they are on display for essentially all campus constituencies for the duration of their visit. Their schedules tend to be daunting, often deliberately, because committees want to know that their next president will have the stamina, the energy, and the resiliency for the 24/7 demands of the job.

Just as they have done throughout the process, successful finalists demonstrate a keen understanding of and interest in the institution. They find the right balance between, on the one hand, making it clear that they do not know enough about the institution's history and culture to lay out any particular plans of action, and on the other hand, answering questions with enough specificity that the campus gains an understanding of how they think and their values. They also give the campus confidence that they understand its external and internal challenges, will listen carefully and be transparent, will manage and enhance the institution's resources, and will work well with all campus constituencies and the board.

The Private Persona

Some candidates fall by the wayside because they reveal a different persona in private from the one they display in public. For example, one finalist who seemed energetic while on campus lost credibility with the search committee when he sat in the back seat when being driven by a student committee member the two hours to and from the airport, speaking only to complain about how tired he was. The committee later enthusiastically embraced the candidate who sat in the front seat with the same student driver. She impressed the committee because she took this occasion to ask the student lots of questions about the college, and as importantly, listen to the answers. Others have been inconsistent in their responses to different audiences, giving the impression that they are playing to their audience.

The Spouse or Partner

In my experience, search committees understand that they are hiring a president, not a presidential couple, and that they are interviewing the candidates and not their spouses or partners. Most committees understand that the days when colleges got two-for-one—that is, a president and unpaid presidential spouse—are no longer the norm. No committee with which I have worked has looked away from a candidate because she or he was single.

Yet, again, spouses and partners do matter if they are especially appealing or if they suggest that they will be problematic. One otherwise engaging spouse worried the committee when she explained that the greatest pleasure she and her husband had was regularly going to the opera. Unfortunately, the college was located in rural America, some two hours away from the nearest city, which had no opera. One couple in a commuting relationship worried the committee because of their plan to travel on alternate weekends to be with one another. What, the committee wondered, if the president's weekend to travel coincided with an important campus event? Another commuting couple, in contrast, took the issue off the table by explaining that the president would be available for all campus events and that her spouse would simply join her whenever possible.

Why Searches Predict Successful Presidencies

Does seeming presidential throughout the extended search process have anything at all to do with whether a person will be successful as a college president? Or to put it another way, does the search process gauge only whether a candidate is good at searches, but not necessarily at being an effective president?

In the end, I have concluded that the search process is a good indicator simply because college presidents need to be able at all times of day or night to walk into a room, sometimes in anxiety-producing situations, with good grace and charm, and engage those who are there. They need to do so whether they are tired or rested, whether they know the people they are meeting or none of them, whether the questions are softballs or sharp arrows. They need to be able to turn meetings into conversations, use humor when appropriate, and always represent their institution well. They need to be well informed before making judgments. They need to be articulate. They need to ask the right questions, lots of them. They need to inspire confidence. Indeed, they need to be able to be responsive to unexpected questions and unexpected situations. In short, even as candidates, they need to appear presidential.

References

American College Presidents Study. Washington, DC: American Council of Education (ACE), 2007.

"ACE Releases First National Census of Chief Academic Officers." Press release for *The CAO Census: A National Profile of Chief Academic Officers*. Washington, DC: American Council of Education, Feb. 9, 2009. http://www.acenet.edu/AM/PrinterTemplate.cfm?Section=HENA&TEMPLATE=/CM/ContentDisplay.cfm&CONTENTID=31044.

Chait, Richard P., Holland, Thomas P., and Taylor, Barbara E. *The Effective Board of Trustees*. New York: ACE Macmillan Series on Higher Education, 1991.

Duane, Daniel. "Eggheads United." *New York Times*, May 5, 2003.

Ekman, Richard. "The Imminent Crisis in College Leadership." *Chronicle of Higher Education*, Sept. 19, 2010. http://chronicle.com/article/The-Imminent-Crisis-in-College/124513.

Foley, Ryan. "U. of Wisconsin-Madison Biggest School to Pick Gay President." *Edge Boston*, May 29, 2008. http://www.edgeboston.com/index.php?ch=news&sc=glbt&sc3=&id=75199.

Gellis, David. "The First Word on Larry Summers." *Harvard Crimson*, May 4, 2001.

Hartley, Harold V. III, and Godin, Eric E. "A Study of Chief Academic Officers of Independent Colleges and Universities." Washington, DC: Council of Independent Colleges, 2010.

Hull, Roger. *Lead or Leave: A Primer for College Presidents and Board Members.* Lanham, MD: Hamilton Books, 2010.

Keohane, Nannerl O. *Thinking About Leadership.* Princeton, NJ: Princeton University Press, 2010.

King, Jacqueline, and Gomez, Gigi G. *On the Pathway to the Presidency: Characteristics of Higher Education's Senior Leadership.* Washington, DC: American Council of Education, 2008.

Lawrence, Francis. *Leadership in Higher Education: Views from the Presidency.* New Brunswick, NJ: Transaction Publishers, 2006.

Lipka, Sara. "New President Gamely Honeymoons with Carleton." *Chronicle of Higher Education,* Nov. 28, 2010.

Liquidity and Credit Risk at Endowed U.S. Universities and Not-for-Profits. Moody's Investor Services, June 14, 2010.

Major Differences: Examining Student Engagement by Field of Study—Annual Results 2010. National Survey of Student Engagement. Bloomington: Indiana University Center for Postsecondary Research, 2010. http://nsse.iub.edu/NSSE_2010_Results/pdf/NSSE_2010_AnnualResults.pdf.

McLaughlin, Judith Block. *Leadership Transitions: The New College President.* San Francisco: Jossey-Bass, 1996.

Morais, Betsy. "IvyGate Presidential Fame Caucus: Ruth Simmons." IvyGate, Feb. 19, 2010.

Morse, Robert J., and Flanigan, Samuel. "How We Calculate the Rankings." *US News & World Report, Best Colleges 2011,* pp. 86-87.

O'Neill, Molly. "On Campus with Dr. Judith Rodin: In an Ivy League of Her Own." *New York Times,* Oct. 20, 1994.

Pryor, John, Hurtado, Sylvia, DeAngelo, Linda, Blake, Laura Palucki, and Tran, Serge. *The American Freshman: National Norms Fall 2010*. Los Angeles: Cooperative Institutional Research Program, Higher Education Research Institute, and UCLA's Graduate School of Education & Information Studies, 2010.

Sanaghan, Patrick H., Goldstein, Larry, and Gavel, Kathleen D. *Presidential Transitions*. Westport, CT: ACE/Praeger Series on Higher Education, 2008.

Sax, Linda J., Astin, Alexander W., Lindholm, Jennifer A., Kom, William S., Saenz, Victor B., and Mahoney, Kathy W. *The American Freshman: National Norms Fall 2003*. Los Angeles: Higher Education Research Institute at UCLA, 2003.

Statement on Government of Colleges and Universities. American Association of University Professors, American Council on Education, and Association of Governing Boards, 1966. http://www.aaup.org/AAUP/pubsres/ policydocs/contents/governancestatement.htm.

Stripling, Jack. "Flagships Just Want to Be Alone." *Chronicle of Higher Education*, Mar. 13, 2011. http://chronicle.com/article/Flagships-Just-Want-to-Be/126696.

Stripling, Jack. "Moody's Probes Colleges on Cash." *Inside Higher Ed*, June 16, 2010. http://www.insidehighered.com/news/2010/06/16/moody's.

Strunk, William, and White, E. B. *The Elements of Style*. New York: Macmillan, 1959.

Summers, Lawrence H. "Remarks at NBER Conference on Diversifying the Science & Engineering Workforce." Jan. 14, 2005. president.harvard.edu/speeches/summers_2005/nber.php.

Tolstoy, Leo. *Anna Karenina*. (Constance Garnett, trans.). New York: Barnes & Noble Classics, 2003, p. 5.

Welsh-Huggins, Andrew. "Ohio State Gets Popular Prez." *USA Today*, July 12, 2007.

Williams, Gabriel. "Celebrity Style: B.E.T. Honors 2010 Show." DRJAYS.com, Feb. 3, 2010.

Resources

Barr, Margaret J., and McClellan, George S. *Budgets and Financial Management in Higher Education.* San Francisco: Jossey-Bass, 2011.

Bolman, Lee G., and Gallos, Joan V. *Reframing Academic Leadership.* San Francisco: Jossey-Bass, 2011.

Bornstein, Rita. *Legitimacy in the Academic Presidency: From Entrance to Exit.* Westport, CT: ACE/Praeger Series on Higher Education, 2003.

Chait, Richard P., Ryan, William P., and Taylor, Barbara E. *Governance as Leadership: Reframing the Work of Nonprofit Boards.* Hoboken, NJ: BoardSource, Inc., and John Wiley and Sons, 2005.

Fullan, Michael, and Scott, Geoff. *Turnaround Leadership for Higher Education.* San Francisco: Jossey-Bass, 2009.

McLaughlin, Judith Block, and Riesman, David. *Choosing a College President: Opportunities and Constraints.* Princeton, NJ: The Carnegie Foundation for the Advancement of Teaching, 1990.

Middaugh, Michael F. *Planning and Assessment in Higher Education: Demonstrating Institutional Effectiveness.* San Francisco: Jossey-Bass, 2009.

Morrill, Richard L. *Assessing Presidential Effectiveness: A Guide for College and University Boards.* Washington, DC: Association of Governing Boards, 2010.

Rosovksy, Henry. *The University: An Owner's Manual*. New York: Norton, 1990.

Sample, Steve B. *The Contrarian's Guide to Leadership*. San Francisco: Jossey-Bass, 2002.

Trachtenberg, Stephen Joel. *Big Man on Campus: A University President Speaks Out on Higher Education*. New York: Touchstone, 2009.

Washburn, Jennifer. *University, Inc*. New York: Basic Books, 2005.

Index

14–16; presidential missteps with budgeting, 10–12; staff suggestions on improving efficiency, 70
Financial strategic planning: borrowing decisions, 87; compliance with government regulations, 87–88; for generating new revenue, 29; hiring lobbyists as part of, 99; institutional values influencing budget, 85–91; long-range, 86–87; as presidential responsibility, 36–37. *See also* Strategic planning
"The First Word on Larry Summers" (Gellis), 106
Fishbowls. *See* President's private/public life
"Flagships Just Want to Be Alone" (Stripling), 28–29
Flanigan, Samuel, 40
Foley, Ryan, 155
Fong, Bobby, 153
Foodservice staff, 41, 136
For-profit auxiliary programs, 41–42
Foundation funding, 98–99
Fundraising: donor relationships driving, 92–93; hiring lobbyists as part of, 99; presidency pleasure through rewards of, 136–137; as president responsibility, 29, 83–84, 100–101; principles of, 93–96; resisting gifts with inappropriate conditions, 93; understanding which areas attract, 91–92
Fundraising donors: alumni, 97; corporations, 99; federal and state funding through grants, 99; foundations, 98–99; parents, 97–99; president stewardship of, 100–101; president's pleasure of working with, 136–137; relationships as driving fundraising, 92–93; trustees, 96–97
Future of college presidency: attracting good people, 162–165;

CAO (chief academic officer) route to, 144–149; changing nature of presidential ranks, 144–152; interest in nontraditional candidates, 149–152; leadership development opportunities for, 161–162; mixed news about candidate pools, 165–166; quest for diversity, 153–161

G
Gavel, Kathleen D., 32
Gay candidates, 154
Gee, Gordon, 106
Gellis, David, 106
GI Bill, 136
Goldstein, Larry, 323
Gomez, Gigi, 153
Grade inflation, 38–39
Greek system, 6–7, 181
Greeley, Horace, 104
Grinnell College, 154
Groundsperson crew, 41, 70, 135–136

H
Harvard Crimson, 106
Harvard Institute for Educational Management (IEM), 161
Harvard Seminar for New Presidents, 114, 115
Harvard University, 29, 107
Hesburgh, Theodore, 29
Higher Education Research Institute (HERI) [UCLA], 38, 89
Higher Education Resource Services Institutes (HERS), 161–162
Holland, Thomas P., 25
"How We Calculate the Ratings" (Morse and Flanigan), 40
Hull, Roger, 35, 87
Humor: during candidate interview, 180; handling rumors with, 115–116
Hurricane Katrina, 75

Search committees: board chair role in, 124; challenges facing internal candidates assessed by, 170–173; considering role of spouse or partners, 112–113; Elizabethtown College profile sent out by, 152; laws against marital status consideration by, 111–112; Ohio Wesleyan University profile send out by, 151–152; retiring presidents' involvement with, 123. *See also* President candidates; President search process; President-elect

Search consultants, 177–178

Senior staff: attracting as president candidates, 165; direct report/follow-up memo communication with, 72; encouraged to think institutionally, 54; fostering competition not collaboration among, 9–10, 71; handling mistakes made by, 72; maximizing president's time with, 79–80; president's relationship with, 70–72; problems created by outgoing presidents for, 121–122; providing clear expectations for, 71–72; trustee interactions with, 51–52; unfavorable personnel decisions on, 77; what incoming presidents need to know about the, 127. *See also* Staff

Sexual harassment, 74

Sexual orientation diversity, 154

Simmons, Ruth, 105–106

The single (unmarried) president, 114–115

Spoke-and-hub management style, 9

Spouses or partners: ability to honor confidentiality, 112; during the campus visit, 189; the role of the, 111–114. *See also* Marital status; Presidents

Staff: attracting as president candidates, 165; custodians, 70; foodservice, 41, 136; groundsperson crew, 41, 70, 135–136; interaction between president and retired, 58; internet monitoring by, 76; maintenance, 41–42; president authority to hire, 65; president's relationship with, 69–70; recognizing the value of good, 69–70; recommendations on president's office, 62–63; as "retention officers," 70; student retention role of, 54; their dedication as pleasure of the presidency, 134–136; trustee interactions with, 51–52; unfavorable personnel decisions on, 77; what incoming presidents need to know about the, 127. *See also* Senior staff

Staley, Thomas F., 85

State government grants, 99

State legislators: advice for presidents on working with, 27–28; declining state appropriations approved by, 29; public institution presidents' relationship with, 26–28; public institutions seeking more autonomy from, 28

Statement on Government of Colleges and Universities, 1966, 67

Strategic planning: board-presidential partnership in, 49–50; overly optimistic, 11; presidential missteps with, 10–11; as presidential responsibility, 30, 36–37; problems with outgoing presidents setting, 118–120; recommendations on developing, 63–64; risk management, 75–76. *See also* Financial strategic planning

Stripling, Jack, 19–20, 28

Student enrollment: redesigning curriculum to increase, 33–34;